ETERNITY IS NOW IN SESSION

ETERNITY
IS NOW
IN SESSION

A RADICAL REDISCOVERY OF WHAT JESUS
REALLY TAUGHT ABOUT SALVATION,
ETERNITY, AND GETTING TO THE GOOD PLACE

JOHN
ORTBERG

TYNDALE
MOMENTUM®

The nonfiction imprint of
Tyndale House Publishers, Inc.

Visit Tyndale online at www.tyndale.com.

Visit Tyndale Momentum online at www.tyndalemomentum.com.

TYNDALE, Tyndale Momentum, and Tyndale's quill logo are registered trademarks of Tyndale House Publishers, Inc. The Tyndale Momentum logo is a trademark of Tyndale House Publishers, Inc. Tyndale Momentum is the nonfiction imprint of Tyndale House Publishers, Inc., Carol Stream, Illinois.

Eternity Is Now in Session: A Radical Rediscovery of What Jesus Really Taught about Salvation, Eternity, and Getting to the Good Place

Designed by Jennifer Phelps

Edited by Jonathan Schindler

For information about special discounts for bulk purchases, please contact Tyndale House Publishers at csresponse@tyndale.com, or call 1-800-323-9400.

Library of Congress Cataloging-in-Publication Data

Names: Ortberg, John, author.
Title: Eternity is now in session : a radical rediscovery of what Jesus really taught
    about salvation, eternity, and getting to the good place / John Ortberg.
Description: Carol Stream, Illinois : Tyndale House Publishers, Inc., 2018. |
    Includes bibliographical references.
Identifiers: LCCN 2018009770 | ISBN 9781496431646 (hc)
Subjects: LCSH: Eternity. | Future life—Christianity. | Salvation—Christianity.
Classification: LCC BT913 .O78 2018 | DDC 236/.21—dc23 LC record available at
    https://lccn.loc.gov/2018009770

Printed in the United States of America

24   23   22   21   20   19   18
7   6   5   4   3   2   1

To Kent Bechler and Danny Wood,
treasured companions on the long journey toward God.

CONTENTS

ARE WE THERE YET?

As leaders of the church, we are in the salvation business.
The whole of the gospel is intent on deliverance.
Our opportunity, and our problem, is making sure we
understand exactly what salvation means. All of it.

DALLAS WILLARD

Are we there yet?

Every parent has heard it.

Every kid has asked it.

Every human being has felt it.

We suffer from destination impatience. We rush through life, always in a hurry. To get to where, we do not know.

The late cardiologist Meyer Friedman coined the phrase "hurry sickness" to describe this rushed, worried, preoccupied, time-poor quality of our lives after his upholsterer noted the unusual pattern of wear on the chairs in his waiting room. Apparently, they had only become worn out along the front edge. With nothing to do other than wait to meet with their cardiologist, people were *literally* sitting on the edge of their seats.

Are we there yet?

Something in us is waiting. For what, we do not know.

Something different? Something better? Sometimes it feels like we've been waiting forever.

In the Christian faith, the deepest and most mysterious expression of what we're waiting for is found in the word *eternity*. God has "set eternity in the human heart," we're told in Ecclesiastes 3:11. We have a haunting sense that there is something more than this transient world. We alone of all creatures know that "all flesh is as grass." But God has set eternity in the human heart.

Are we there yet?

Most of us think of eternity as an endless duration of time. And yet we hunger for more than just an infinite continuation of life as we now experience it, with all its sufferings and disappointments. In fact, the fear of unending existence carries its own label—*apeirophobia*—and can be as unsettling as the thought of death.[1]

But in her book *Images of Salvation in the New Testament*, Brenda Colijn writes that the eternal life the Bible talks about is *not* primarily marked by its duration. Eternal life is "qualitatively different from mortal human life. It is 'the life by which God Himself lives.'"[2] It is "primarily qualitative rather than quantitative."[3] "'Eternal' describes the kind of life one has in Christ."[4]

Which means eternal life isn't just about the future. We can have it now. It's not just about there. We can have it here.

Most important, it's not something we simply receive through a transaction that arranges for our future destination. It's something we experience now through becoming Jesus' disciples, which death is then unable to stop.

This means many of us will have to think differently about the Good News that Jesus brought.

According to Boston University professor of religion Stephen Prothero, it is the notion of an "arrangement" for getting into eternal life someday that sets Christianity apart from other religions. In his book *God Is Not One*, Prothero defines Christianity as "the way of salvation." He describes the usual Christian message: "Sinners cannot be admitted to heaven or granted eternal life"; therefore, "anyone who hears this story [the gospel], confesses her sins, and turns to Jesus for forgiveness, can be saved," which results in "go[ing] to heaven." He goes on to say, "Today the price of admission to the Christian family continues to be orthodoxy (right thought) rather than orthopraxy," actually doing what Jesus said.[5] In other words, Christians are people who believe the right things and will therefore be allowed into heaven when they die.

This view calls to mind the climax of the movie *Monty Python and the Holy Grail*, when King Arthur and his knights come to the castle they've been seeking. Lying between them and the castle is a bottomless abyss, and a wizened old bridge keeper guards the only bridge that allows access. If they can give the correct answer to his questions, they are allowed to cross. If not, they are cast into the abyss.

I believe this is how many people today think about salvation. When we die, we are either headed for the castle (heaven) or the abyss (hell), and "salvation" is knowing the right answer so that God has to allow us to cross the bridge.

The problem is, Jesus doesn't talk about salvation that way. He doesn't talk about *eternal life* that way either. In fact, Jesus—and the entire New Testament, for that matter—defines *eternal life* only once, with great precision, and in a way that has been largely lost in our day: "This is eternal life, that they may know you, the only true God, and Jesus Christ whom you have sent" (John 17:3, NRSV).

Eternal Life = Knowing God.

Notice that Jesus doesn't say "that they may know *about* you." He says "that they may *know* you."

Philosophers distinguish between knowledge by description and knowledge by acquaintance.[6] For example, I might be able to *describe* Moscow because I've read about it in books and seen it in movies, but I know *by acquaintance* what Rockford, Illinois feels like on a hot August night and what it smells like after a thunderstorm. I know the sound of a tennis ball bouncing on the courts of East High School. I know its hopes and divisions and fears, and I know Stockholm Inn Swedish Pancakes because Rockford was my home.

Knowledge by acquaintance *includes* description but goes

far deeper. It is interactive and participatory and experiential. The kind of "knowing God" that is eternal life is an interactive relationship where I experience God's presence and favor and power in my real life on this earth.

To know God is to live in a rich, moment-by-moment, gratitude-soaked, participatory life together.

To know God means to know myself as his beloved friend as a gift of grace.

To know God means to know what Paul called "the power of his resurrection" (Philippians 3:10) in the details and tasks and challenges of my daily, ordinary life.

This is eternal life. It is not something far away in outer space that we can only hope to experience after we die. It is not simply being able to give the right answers at church, affirming the right doctrines, or achieving the minimum entrance requirements to cross over the bridge and get into heaven.

On the contrary, it's something much bigger and far more amazing. The gospel Jesus preached is the Good News that this eternal kind of life is available *now*. By grace. Through Jesus. Forever and beyond death. "Eternal life in the individual does not begin after death, but at the point where God touches the individual with redeeming grace and draws them into a life interactive with himself and his kingdom."[7]

I have a sign on the back wall of my office that I look at first thing every morning when I sit down at my desk. In large block letters, it echoes something my good friend Dallas Willard used to say: "Eternity Is Now in Session."

God is not waiting for eternity to begin. God lives in it right now. It is the interactive fellowship and joy that exists between Father, Son, and Holy Spirit. Eternity is rolling right along, and we are invited to be part of it—*now*.

Certainly, as long as we're in this world, we have much to wait for. Are we there yet? Of course not. Death still robs us of those we love, children still go hungry, refugees have no place to live. We lose our jobs or our dreams or our loved ones. Our bodies age and decay. Every day when I look at the mirror, I'm reminded I'm not there yet. Paul wrote that creation itself is groaning for the day when it will be "liberated from its bondage to decay" (Romans 8:21). Amazingly, even the Spirit of God groans for this (verse 26). To anyone who wonders, along with an old neurotic Jack Nicholson movie character, "What if this is as good as it gets?" Paul says that not only we but all creation will one day taste the freedom and glory of the children of God. "What would become of us," asked John Calvin, "if we did not take our stand on hope?"[8]

And yet, in another way, we *are* there. Or rather, *there* has come *here*. In the midst of our groaning, eternal life has slipped into our temporal world now through the carpenter of Nazareth. In the midst of disappointment and decay, the Sustainer comes alongside me. In the midst of loneliness, a Friend comes who will not let me go. In the midst of the valley of the shadow of death, I will fear no evil, for he is with me. Eternity has invaded time. "There"—life in God's presence and power—has come here. No one yet knows how deeply humanity in this world can enter into the peace and love of eternity. You can make your life a Great Experiment in this adventure.

Dallas once wrote, "We must . . . do nothing less than engage in a radical rethinking of the Christian conception of salvation."[9] I think he's right. Somewhere along the way, the power and the promise of the gospel has been lost. We've shrunk it down by making it solely about going to heaven when we die, and in doing so, we've shrunk God down too. We have often preached a gospel that does not naturally call for "knowing God," a gospel that does not naturally call for disciples.

But what if we stopped thinking about the gospel as simply the minimum entrance requirements to get into heaven?

What if we stopped thinking about eternal life as something we can only experience after we die?

What if we stopped thinking of Christians as people who *know about* God and instead focused on becoming disciples who are learning to *know* God?

What if salvation isn't mostly about getting us into heaven but about getting heaven into us?

Much of the way we're taught to view eternal life is as a destination we reach, and until we get there, we're like anxious kids on a long car trip asking, "Are we there yet?" We think we're just biding time until we get there, when the real enjoyment will begin. But what if we're missing out along the way?

This book contrasts two ways of thinking about Jesus' gospel. The more common version is thought to involve how people ensure they will go to heaven when they die. It's about how to go from "down here" to "up there." It usually involves affirming certain beliefs or praying a particular prayer that is thought to make a person a "Christian."

The other understanding is that the gospel announces the availability of life under God's reign and power *now*. It's about "up there" coming "down here." By grace. Through Jesus. Transcending death. To all who will. For the sake of the world.

The first version tends to produce consumers of Jesus' merit. The second tends to produce disciples of Jesus' Way.

I believe the latter version is the correct one, the one that Jesus taught, the one that "snapped history into B.C. and A.D. as if it were a dry twig."[10] He is still recruiting people for this, the great journey of inner change and outer purpose.

Maybe he's recruiting you.

Are we there yet?

It's time to "engage in a radical rethinking of the Christian conception of salvation."

Eternity is now in session.

PART 1

RETHINKING SALVATION

BREAKING NEWS

[The Widow Douglas] told me all about the bad place,
and I said I wished I was there. . . . She said it was wicked to say
what I said . . . she was going to live so as to go to the
good place. . . . She said all a body would have to do there was
to go around all day long with a harp and sing, forever
and ever. . . . Well, I couldn't see no advantage in going where
she was going, so I made up my mind I wouldn't try for it.

MARK TWAIN, *The Adventures of Huckleberry Finn*

Most human beings believe in an afterlife. And in most cases, this belief involves a good place and a bad place.

If you're a good person, and you embrace the right beliefs, you go to the good place. If you're not, and you don't, you go to the bad place. Seems simple enough.

If you were to ask people what they believe heaven will be like, some would halfheartedly describe it like the Widow Douglas's harp community. Others think of it as an eternal pleasure factory, where you are always happy, you have amazing superpowers, and you can do whatever you want. In the movie *Defending Your Life*, heaven is depicted as a place where you can eat all the carbs and fat you want because they have no calories. The TV series *The Good Place* features a utopian afterlife where angel Ted Danson allows only "good people." In the initial plot twist, the central character is allowed in by accident and has to fake being good. In the season's final plot twist, it turns out that Ted Danson is not an angel (should have seen that one coming) and the Good Place is actually the Bad Place.

Most people think heaven is a place where anybody would *love* to spend eternity as long as they're allowed in. This view of heaven leads people to wonder, *Why* doesn't *God let more people in?*

The problem with these views of heaven is that they're not true. People are taking their picture of heaven from movies rather than thoughtful, sober, grown-up reflection on what Jesus said. "Movie heaven" is pretty much a pleasure factory that anybody would enjoy as long as they were allowed in.

But the life after death that Jesus describes is very different from "movie heaven." Here's the main truth to know about heaven: heaven will be life with God.

In fact, in heaven, it will be impossible to avoid God.

It's not like heaven is an immense place and you have to track God down somewhere, like finding the Wizard of Oz. Heaven does not contain God; God contains heaven. So becoming the kind of person who *wants* heaven—uninterrupted life with God—is a problem because I often want freedom to do things I don't want God to see. Real heaven means life where my every thought, deed, and word lie ceaselessly open to God. For eternity.

Have you ever committed a sexual sin? I'll bet you didn't do it while your mother was watching you. That would have taken all the fun out of it. In order to commit sin and enjoy it, you have to be someplace your mother isn't. In heaven, there is no place where God is not. Once you're in heaven, there is nowhere to run to for a quick sin. If you want to gossip, hoard, judge, self-promote, overindulge, or be cynical, where will you go?

Dallas Willard writes of a time his two-and-a-half-year-old granddaughter wanted to play in the forbidden mud, so she kept saying to her grandmother, "Don't look at me, Nana." Thus "the tender soul of a little child shows us how necessary it is to us that we be unobserved in our wrong."[1] That's why the promise of hiddenness sells. "What happens in Vegas stays in Vegas." This is perhaps the *real* sinner's prayer, offered before every forbidden act, word, and thought: "Don't look at me, God." In heaven that prayer can be neither offered nor answered.

In other words, heaven is the kind of place where people who want to sin would be miserable. A nonsmoking restaurant is great if you're a nonsmoker but miserable to a nicotine addict. What brings joy to one creature may torture another. C. S. Lewis once wrote that "a heaven for mosquitoes and a hell for men could very conveniently be combined."[2]

Heaven is a certain kind of community where humility and honesty and servanthood and generosity of spirit are as predictable as gravity is here. As John Henry Newman wrote, "Heaven is not for everyone: it is an acquired taste."[3]

People often criticize Christianity because they think it envisions heaven as an exclusive club that everyone desperately wants to get into and that God is trying to keep people out of. The reality that Jesus taught, however, is that no one really wants heaven.

The hymn "Rock of Ages" has a telling line:

Be of sin the double cure;
Save from wrath and make me pure.

It's not hard to want the "save from wrath" part of the cure. God was so willing to save us from wrath that he sent Jesus to the cross so that he could experience ultimate spiritual death in our place. Anyone would want to be saved from wrath. We're often a little more ambivalent about "make me pure."[4]

Our issue with heaven is not so much about getting in; it's about becoming the kind of person for whom heaven would be an appropriate and welcome setting. If I don't want the unceasing presence of God in my life now, how could I truly want an eternity in the ceaseless presence of God, where the possibility of any sinful action or thought—no matter how desirable—is forever cut off?

If that's the case, who *will* get in?

If you ever find yourself anxious about "getting in," the best thought I know is not about what arrangement can take away your anxiety but about God. And the thought is this: God will do the absolute best he can by every human being for all eternity. Including you. In light of his Father's goodness, Jesus advised, "Do not worry about tomorrow" (Matthew 6:34). And if God can take care of one tomorrow, he can take care of an eternity of them.

Surely the message that God gave his Son to die on a cross for our sins is the ultimate statement of his limitless desire to forgive and restore human beings. Dallas Willard put it like this: "I am thoroughly convinced that God will let everyone into heaven who, in his considered opinion, can stand it."[5]

That statement often provokes surprise or a chuckle. But if you stop to think about it, it must be true. Why else would God send his Son to die on our behalf?

The problem is that "standing it" may be more difficult than we imagine—especially for those of us hoping for the eternal pleasure factory. That is why, in *The Problem of Pain*, C. S. Lewis writes that "the doors of hell are locked on the *inside*."[6] Hell is the absence of God, and more people want that than you think. I suspect that's why we sometimes speak of only a stairway to heaven but a highway to hell.

There is some good news, though. Eternal life is far more than getting into heaven. Remember, eternal life is *qualitative*—it makes a difference in the *kind* of life we live—more than it is quantitative. And Jesus taught about that life. More than getting us into heaven, he taught how to get heaven into us.

THE GOOD NEWS

You can tell a lot about people by where they get their news. If people are on one side of the political spectrum, they might get their news from one source; if they're on the other side, they might get it from another source.

Where do you get your news?

Jesus was, among other things, in the news-announcing business. That may sound odd; we often think of news as a modern invention. Yet we read that "Jesus went throughout Galilee, *teaching* in their synagogues, *preaching* the good *news* of the kingdom, and healing every disease and sickness among the people. *News* about him spread all over Syria" (Matthew 4:23-24, emphasis added).

There's a key distinction here that we can miss. Jesus *teaches*—he gives instruction or advice on how to live. But he also *preaches*, or proclaims. Today we associate preaching with churches and telling people what to do. But *preaching* wasn't used that way in Jesus' time. It wasn't even a religious word. It was a "news" word.

Jesus went around announcing that something had happened. And it wasn't just news; it was *good* news. That's what the word *gospel* means.

Most people have heard of the word *gospel*. But most people—even most church people—do not know the gospel that Jesus *himself* announced.

So what *is* the Good News that Jesus himself proclaimed?

When that question was first posed to me, I had been a pastor for many years. I had been through seminary and then some. I was a "licensed minister of the gospel," and if you are licensed in something, you should understand it. Yet I had never thought about *Jesus* preaching a gospel. I had thought of the gospel as something that got invented after he died.

But Jesus *did* have a gospel. The New Testament writers are very clear about it. And if Jesus thought something was the biggest news in history, it is unthinkable that people who follow him don't know it.

Mark summarizes Jesus' gospel carefully at the beginning of Jesus' ministry: "After John was put in prison, Jesus went into Galilee, proclaiming the good news [gospel] of God. 'The time has come,' he said. 'The kingdom of God has come near. Repent and believe the good news!'" (Mark 1:14-15).

After choosing his disciples, Jesus "called the Twelve together, he gave them power and authority to drive out all demons and to cure diseases, and he sent them out to preach the kingdom of God" (Luke 9:1-2).

After Jesus rose from the dead, "he appeared to them over a period of forty days and spoke about the kingdom of God" (Acts 1:3).

And in the last glimpse we have of the early church in the book of Acts, Paul "boldly and without hindrance . . . preached the kingdom of God" (Acts 28:31).

Jesus' good news—his *gospel*—is simply this: the Kingdom of God has now, through Jesus, become available for ordinary human beings to live in.

It's here. Now. You can live in it if you want to.

This good news was ultimately vindicated by his death and resurrection and has since gone viral, but it is still Jesus' gospel.

New Testament scholar Matthew Bates notes that from the earliest days of the church, the accounts of Jesus' life were not titled "The Gospel *of* Mark," "The Gospel *of* Matthew," and so on. Instead they were titled "The gospel *according to* Mark" and "The gospel *according to* Matthew."[7] The idea here is that there is only one gospel, and it belongs to Jesus. It was first expressed by him. It is the gospel *of* Jesus. Matthew, Mark, Luke, and John (and Peter and Paul, too, for that matter) were simply writing about the gospel that Jesus articulated and made possible.

Which raises a question: What is the gospel according to *you*? We all—religious or not—build our lives on some gospel, some "good news" that we believe can redeem our existence. Maybe it's money or success or reputation or health or marriage. *Everybody* has a gospel.

This is Jesus' gospel: God is present here and now. God is acting. You can revise your plans for living around this cosmic opportunity to daily experience God's favor and power.

Some people teach that the only real reason Jesus came to earth was to die on the cross. But death on the cross was only one part of his mission. His overall mission was to be the Kingdom bringer.[8]

His one gospel was the gospel of the availability of the Kingdom.

His one purpose was to model the reality of that Kingdom in his life, death, and resurrection.

His one command was to pursue the Kingdom.

His one plan was for his people to extend the Kingdom.

He invites you, as a gracious gift, to become an agent of the Kingdom—to experience God's reign in your own life, body, and will and then to become a conduit of God's power, joy, and love to bruised and bleeding humanity all around you.

Jesus himself had a gospel to proclaim, and unless we begin with that gospel and take it as our central framework, clarified and deepened by the Crucifixion and Resurrection, we are apt to distort the gospel into a backstage, all-access pass to heaven. If we do not start with the gospel Jesus taught, we will end up with a gospel he did *not* teach. The gospel of Jesus' Kingdom offers the salvation of despairing individuals and the healing of systemic injustice. It is the hope of the world.

Yet millions of people who claim his name could not tell you what the Kingdom is.

We don't use the word *Kingdom* often anymore. So let's start there.

WELCOME TO THE KINGDOM

Everyone has a kingdom—in the biblical sense.

Your kingdom is that little sphere in which what you say goes. Your kingdom is the "range of [y]our effective will."[9]

People learn they were made to have kingdoms early on. It's why we don't like to be told what to do. One of my wife's favorite expressions is "You're not the boss of me." It's one of my favorites too.

What is a two-year-old's favorite word? *No.* Their second favorite? *Mine.* They're learning they have a kingdom. That's kingdom language.

On car trips, little kids asked to "share" the backseat will usually draw an invisible line. In doing so, they're saying, "You'd better not cross over. This is *my* kingdom." They begin to defend their kingdoms. But Dad thinks the car is *his* kingdom. He warns the kids to settle down and sends his hand into the backseat. The kids shrink into the corner. Comedian Ken Davis advises that when this happens, "a touch on the brakes brings them right into play." Thy kingdom come.

My kingdom is the range of my effective will. It's the sphere where things go the way I want them to go.

Having a kingdom is a good thing. It's part of what God made you for: "Then God said, 'Let us make humankind in our image, according to our likeness, and let them have dominion'" (Genesis 1:26, NRSV). "Dominion" is kingdom language.

My family was taking a walk on a path through some hills. A man whose house was on the path came out of his house and asked us what our dog's name was. I thought he was being friendly.

Suddenly he screamed at us that we were on private property. He unleashed a barrage of profanity-laced hostility that caught us all off guard in its meanness.

Whose kingdom was he living in?

That man was living in what might be called the "kingdom of self." *This is* my *kingdom. I'll guard it. I won't share it. If you violate my kingdom, I'll kill you.* We had trespassed on his kingdom.

On earth, all our little kingdoms intersect and merge and form larger kingdoms—families, corporations, nations, and economic, political, and cultural systems. We could call that whole conglomeration the "kingdom of the earth." And that kingdom is junked up by sin.

Let's do a contrast study for a moment.

Jesus says there is a domain called the "Kingdom of God." It is the range of God's effective will. It is wherever God's will is done. It is the sphere in which everything that happens meets with God's approval and delight. Everything is precisely as God wants it to be—where the greatest humble themselves like little children. There are no big shots. No arrogant egos. No one ever has an anxious thought. Every encounter between people causes them to walk away with more joy than they had before they met. As the apostle Paul says, "The kingdom of God is not a matter of eating and drinking, but of righteousness, peace and joy in the Holy Spirit" (Romans 14:17). Watching over this whole realm as its greatest servant and most joyful caretaker is the magnificent God—the Father of Jesus—who is endlessly celebrated for his infinite, self-giving love.

This, Jesus said, is the Kingdom of God. It exists. Right now. People you know and love who trusted God and have died and gone before us are immersed in this reality right now.

Then there is the "kingdom of the earth." How's that going?

Violence. Betrayal. Thousands of babies dying daily due to malnutrition. Women being sexually assaulted or marginalized or objectified by men. People killing others in the name of religion. God's creation getting polluted. Vows of fidelity being broken. Racial injustice constantly smoldering and often exploding. Culture wars. The politicization of almost everything. Cynicism and fear and depression and isolation. Who does it look like is running the show here?

Things in the kingdom of the earth are not going well. There is not much good news for the poor or weak or old or plain or uneducated or vulnerable.

But Jesus has a plan. He describes it in the world's most famous prayer:

Our Father, who art in Heaven,
Hallowed be thy name.

Thy kingdom come,
Thy will be done on earth as it is in heaven.

In other words, "Here's my plan. I'm going to bring *this* down *here*."

Like a lot of Christians, I grew up praying the "Beam me up, Scotty" prayer from the old Star Trek series. I thought we were supposed to ask God to get us out of this messed-up earth so we could go to heaven.

But Jesus taught a different prayer. Not "Get me out of here so I can go up there." But "Make up there come down here." "Make things down here run the way they do up there."

Jesus told us to ask God to bring heaven—"*your* kingdom," "*your* will"—down here to my office, my neighborhood, my small group, my family, my country. Starting with my life, my body, my little kingdom.

Jesus' gospel involves the greatest offer of all time. The salvation of your whole life, both now *and* then. Not just getting you into heaven but getting heaven into you. When you get what Jesus is offering, it's like finding treasure in a field that you'd sell everything to possess and laugh all the way to the bank. If it were a late-night TV infomercial, you'd call without delay.

It is *good news*.

The great question is this: Do you really believe it can happen? Do you really believe that the Kingdom of God can be established on this earth, starting with you?

Many people do not understand that this was Jesus' message, his plan, his good news. Even people who are actively involved in church life were taught to pray, "Beam me up."

But Jesus never told anybody to pray, "Get me out of here so I can go up there." He said we were to ask God to establish his Kingdom where we are.

Jesus' gospel is not about something that might happen sometime in the future. It has already begun. In him. In hiddenness. In sacrificial love. Right in the midst of the kingdoms that oppose it.

You may wonder, *If the Kingdom has come in Jesus, why is the earth still a mess? Why are pain and suffering still with us?* And the answer—which took the early church decades to come to grips with—is that other "kingdoms" still remain. Other wills that are opposed to God's will are still present. Thank God, because one of those stubborn wills is mine. One day all opposition will end. But it endures now because God chooses to act not with coercive power but in suffering love.

When Jesus was born, Rome had a gospel. An old Roman inscription read, "The birthday of the god [referring to Caesar Augustus] was the beginning for the world of the glad tidings [Good News, gospel] that have come to men through him."

The gospel of Jesus is a claim that Rome's "good news"— a "good news" purchased by violence and fear—is fake news.

No merely human kingdom can redeem and transform the earth. Only King Jesus can do that.

His ultimate success is certain. And if you want, you can be a part of his Kingdom.

Right here. Right now.

BREAKING IT DOWN

Bringing up there down here is God's project. "Salvation belongs to our God" (Revelation 7:10). One day he will complete it. The promise of the Bible is not that in eternity we will be disembodied spirits living in a cloud-furnished, pearly-gated, gold-bricked spiritual retirement community. It's also not that we will be stuck in a never-ending church service. The promise is that resurrection will come, and God's creation will be made glorious. Our destiny, a good friend of mine used to say, is to be part of a tremendously creative team effort, under unimaginably splendid leadership, on an inconceivably vast scale, with ever-increasing cycles of productivity and fulfillment, and that is what "eye has not seen and ear has not heard" in the prophetic vision.[10]

Theologian Jürgen Moltmann distinguished two kinds of futures: *futurum* and *adventus*. *Futurum* is the kind of future that human beings can explain and hope to manage; *adventus* is a future that breaks into history from the outside. The end of history, Moltmann said, is adventus. It will happen when *God* comes.[11]

We wait for this. We are not in control of it. When human beings try to enforce utopia on one another, bad things happen.

But waiting doesn't mean inactivity. We are not in charge, but we are not idle. We are engaged. We become a part of God's project. Every time you bring a slice of this up-there life down here, the Kingdom of God breaks into all the messed-up kingdoms of this world.

Every time you are in conflict with someone, when you want to hurt them, gossip about them, avoid them, but instead you go to them and seek reconciliation and forgiveness, the Kingdom is breaking into this world.

Every time you have a chunk of money and you decide to give sacrificially to somebody who is hungry or homeless or poor, the Kingdom is breaking into the world.

Every time somebody who has an addiction wants to partner with God so badly that they're willing to stop hiding, acknowledge the truth, and get help from a loving community, the Kingdom is breaking into the world.

Every time a workaholic parent decides to stop idolizing their job and rearranges their life to begin to love and care for the little children entrusted to them, the Kingdom is breaking into the world.

This good news happens through Jesus. Jesus himself—through his incarnation—is literally "up there" coming "down here." "The Word became flesh and made his dwelling among us" (John 1:14).

The Good News is *not* that we're called to do these things on our own, as though we're being given a longer to-do list. The

Good News is that a power has become available to increasingly turn us into the kind of people who *naturally and recreationally* do such things.

That's why when Jesus goes to Zacchaeus's house and Zacchaeus gives half his possessions to the poor and agrees to pay back all he has cheated four times over, Jesus says, "Today salvation has come to this house" (Luke 19:9). That doesn't just mean that Zacchaeus will be with God when he dies (although of course he will!). It means Jesus has come to this house, that up there is coming down here, because now—through Jesus— a corrupt tax collector has become a Kingdom bringer, the poor are being helped, the cheated are receiving justice, and God's will is being done on earth as it is in heaven.

The gospel—including the Good News of the Cross itself— means the renewal of all things. Miroslav Volf writes, "The cross is not forgiveness pure and simple, but *God's setting aright* the world of injustice and deception."[12] That is what the gospel announces. Starting with Zacchaeus. And you and me.

2

THE MINIMUM ENTRANCE REQUIREMENTS

It is by grace you have been saved, through faith—
and this is not from yourselves, it is the gift of God—
not by works, so that no one can boast. For we are God's
handiwork, created in Christ Jesus to do good works,
which God prepared in advance for us to do.

EPHESIANS 2:8-10

"I was saved from sin when I was going on thirteen. But not really saved."

So begins Langston Hughes's brief, poignant essay "Salvation." He describes being deposited on the mourners' bench at the front row of his auntie Reed's church during a series of revival services.

> My aunt told me that when you were saved you saw
> a light, and something happened to you inside! And
> Jesus came into your life! And God was with you from
> then on! She said you could see and hear and feel Jesus

in your soul. I believed her. I had heard a great many old people say the same thing and it seemed to me they ought to know. So I sat there calmly in the hot, crowded church, waiting for Jesus to come to me.[1]

The preacher preached a sermon of moans and shouts, of dire pictures of hell and plaintive cries for lost lambs: "Won't you come? Won't you come to Jesus? Young lambs, won't you come?"

And Langston waited.

Finally all the young people had gone to the altar and were saved, but one boy and me. He was a rounder's son named Westley. Westley and I were surrounded by sisters and deacons praying. It was very hot in the church, and getting late now. Finally Westley said to me in a whisper . . . "I'm tired o' sitting here. Let's get up and be saved." So he got up and was saved.[2]

Langston was left all alone on the mourners' bench, waiting for a Jesus who did not come. The minister pleaded. His aunt sobbed for him. The congregation prayed. Finally, out of shame and embarrassment and fear, Langston decided he'd better lie too, and say that Jesus had come, and get up, and get saved.

The church loudly rejoiced. But inside, Langston quietly died.

That night, for the last time in my life but one—for I was a big boy twelve years old—I cried. I cried, in bed alone, and couldn't stop. I buried my head under the quilts, but my aunt heard me. She woke up and told my uncle I was crying because the Holy Ghost had come into my life, and because I had seen Jesus. But I was really crying because I couldn't bear to tell her that I had lied, that I had deceived everybody in the church, that I hadn't seen Jesus, and that now I didn't believe there was a Jesus anymore, since he didn't come to help me.[3]

Langston is not alone. Many people who seek God or hunger for the spiritual may find themselves, like Langston, frustrated with what they've heard about "how to be saved." In some traditions people may be told that if they pray a particular "salvation prayer," it should put their soul concerns to rest, but they are troubled when that doesn't happen. The satirical website the *Babylon Bee* posted an article headlined "Bible Lacking Sinner's Prayer Returned for Full Refund." In it, a fictional disgruntled customer says, "I searched that Bible through and through and couldn't find anything about a magic prayer I could lead people to say in order to instantly get them into the Kingdom and have them be forevermore secure in their eternal salvation no matter what their life looks like afterward."[4]

Many find that, like Langston, once they pray the magic

prayer, they don't feel the dramatic inner change they expected to experience. They wonder if they did it right. So they pray the prayer again the next night, the next week, the next year. They're troubled that perhaps they're not really "in."

The problem is not that they said the prayer incorrectly. The problem is that their definition of salvation is too small. The problem is that they're defining salvation as having their entrance application to heaven accepted rather than receiving life from Jesus from one moment to the next.

It is certainly and wonderfully true that many people find that their life with God starts through responding to an altar call, or praying a prayer of forgiveness, or crying out for mercy in a rescue mission. It is certainly and wonderfully true that God's capacity to save us is not dependent on our ability to correctly define salvation.

It is also certainly and wonderfully true that the message of Jesus and his early followers is not just the forgiveness of sins that allows us to escape the bad place and go to the good place. It is newness of life. To be sure, this new life includes forgiveness, but it includes so much more. This is why the primary word used as a synonym for salvation in the New Testament is *life*:

I have come that they may have life, and have it to the full.
JOHN 10:10

Whoever has the Son has life.

1 JOHN 5:12

Because of his great love for us, God, who is rich in mercy, made us alive with Christ even when we were dead in transgressions.

EPHESIANS 2:4-5

In the New Testament, the terms *salvation* and *eternal life* and *Kingdom of God* all speak to this same life-altering reality that we grasp by becoming disciples of Jesus.

We see this particularly well in Mark 10, when a rich man asks Jesus what he must do "to inherit *eternal life*" (verse 17). Jesus equates this with "enter[ing] *the kingdom of God*" (he uses this phrase three times in verses 23-25). The disciples respond, "Who then can be *saved*?" (verse 26).

As we see in this exchange, to have eternal life is to enter the Kingdom of God is to be saved.

When the rich man asks Jesus how to do that, Jesus does not say, "Pray this prayer, and then you can go on your way." He doesn't say, "Believe the right things about me, and then you'll get into heaven when you die." Rather, he tells the man to dethrone money and enthrone Jesus—not to earn forgiveness but to live in the reality of the Kingdom. "Your will be done . . ."

Salvation isn't about getting you into heaven; it's about getting heaven into you.

It's not about relocation; it's about transformation.

It's not about what God wants to do *to* you; it's about what God wants to do *in* you.

It's about allowing Jesus' Kingdom life to permeate our little lives one moment, one choice at a time.

ELITE STATUS

In many church circles, the standard question to determine whether someone is "saved" has historically been "If you should die tonight, how do you know you'd go to heaven?" Usually, when people ask this question, what they are really asking is "How do you know for sure that you have satisfied the minimum entrance requirements for getting into heaven when you die?" They might not use those exact words, but ultimately, that's what they mean. "Have you done enough to push you over the boundary line from hell into heaven?"

"Saving faith" becomes the minimum amount you have to believe so that, if you believe it, God has to let you into heaven. Other beliefs then are optional as far as salvation is concerned.

Can you imagine Jesus himself teaching this? "Believing that all I teach is true—*that's* optional. Believing that I can run your life and allowing me to do so—*that's* optional. Intending to actually obey me—*that's* optional. As long as you believe that my death paid for your sins, you don't need to worry about doing what I've said as far as heaven is concerned."

Or imagine Jesus tacking a salvation caveat onto the Sermon on the Mount: "Everyone who hears these words of mine and puts them into practice is like a wise man who built his house on the rock. Everyone who hears these words of mine and does not put them into practice is like a foolish man who built his house on sand. But just to be clear—you don't have to worry about actually doing anything I say as long as you believe my death pays for your sins."

It is unimaginable that Jesus would think or say this. The reason Jesus called for us to obey him is not so that we can earn our way into heaven. It is because, as George MacDonald put it, "to obey Jesus is to ascend to the pinnacle of my being."[5] Obedience—rightly understood—is what a saved life looks like from the inside. Saving faith is faith that allows me to engage in interactive, grace-powered life with him beginning here and now, which death will then be powerless to interrupt. It is faith that allows me to know union with Christ.

Rankin Wilbourne writes, "Union with Christ is not an idea to be understood, but a new reality to be lived, through faith."[6] If union is the ultimate goal of our life with Christ, and it is, of course it includes trusting that Jesus is right about everything. Of course it includes asking him to take over my little life.

Likewise, when we speak of "trusting Christ for our salvation," what we often really mean is trusting an *arrangement* he made to get us into the good place when we die. Ironically, people sometimes believe they can trust in the arrangement Jesus made without actually trusting Jesus himself—everything he said about money and sex and anger and prayer and God. But we are not called to trust an arrangement. As George MacDonald writes, "Paul *glories* in the cross, but he does not *trust* in the cross: he trusts in the living Christ and his living father."[7]

To "trust Jesus" in the Gospels simply means to think he is right—about *everything*—and therefore to be ready to do what he says, not as a means of getting into the good place but as the best advice from the wisest person possible. In fact, it's only as we seek to do what Jesus says—to be generous and forgiving and radically truthful—that we discover the Kingdom he talks about is real and can be trusted. This is the "Great Experiment" that Jesus himself invites us to run: "Anyone who chooses to do the will of God will find out whether my teaching comes from God or whether I speak on my own" (John 7:17).

Now we begin to understand why the "minimum entrance requirements" question is such a problematic approach to salvation. It speculates on the bare minimum someone could do or believe and still eke their way into heaven (information Jesus does not offer us). Imagine saying to Jesus, "I trust that you've deposited merit in my heavenly bank account, and I will consume your merit to get in, but I don't trust you enough to actually do what you've said in my everyday life. I'll use your blood to avoid hell, but I'd like to retain control of my own life." That kind of trust would be both insulting and nonsensical.

Let's consider another, more temporal example.

Let's say I acquire elite status in an airline's frequent-flyer program and I ask, "What's the bare minimum I have to do to maintain my status?" This is an altogether proper question, because there is no connection between the perks I desire and the person I'm becoming. Anyone would want better seats, nicer food, linen napkins, red carpets. It is an objective, forensic, legal status. The airline will even keep track of my miles to make sure I *do* satisfy the minimum requirements.

But imagine if I had said to Nancy on our wedding day, "I want to know: what's the *absolute least* I can do to stay married to you? What's the lowest level of commitment, the fewest affirmations, the smallest promises, the highest level of ignorance permissible? What are the minimum requirements for maintaining my husband status?"

It would have been a very short ceremony.

Marriage as God designed it is not just a *legal* status. It is a personal, spiritual, relational reality where the relationship itself is the "perk." Not just anybody wants to be married. It requires fidelity, a hard limit on sexual partners, vulnerability, servanthood, commitment, and giving up the remote control.

Are there minimum requirements for remaining married? For sure. Marriages end every day. But these minimum requirements are not fully knowable in advance, and they depend upon the heart. If you really want the marriage, the minimum requirements will take care of themselves. And if you don't really want the marriage, the minimum requirements won't matter.

Ephesians 5:31-32 says, "'For this reason a man will leave his father and mother and be united to his wife, and the two will become one flesh.' This is a profound mystery—but I am talking about Christ and the church."

Salvation as described in Scripture is much more like a marriage than it is like an airline status. We don't need just the benefit of a future salvation; we need the perks of the relationship here and now.

PARDON ME?

"In our world, something is terribly wrong and cries out to be put right."[8] This thought, though written by a theologian, is more often expressed in our day by poets and playwrights and novelists and musicians.

Hunger and poverty haven't gone away. Powerful celebrities assault women. The climate gets warmer. Marriages break up. Religion divides people. Politics can't get any uglier (at least we hope not).

But it's not just the world. Something is terribly wrong *in me*. I'm afraid, alone, aging, arrogant, anxious. And I haven't even gotten to the *B* words yet.

You can divide the mess that is my life into two categories:

problems outside of me and problems inside of me. Problems outside of me are problems that involve my job, my relationships, my bank account, my neighborhood, my nation—even my health. The problems inside of me have names like ego, addiction, insatiable desire, envy, coldheartedness, and deceit.

G. K. Chesterton wrote, "Whatever else men have believed, they have all believed that there is something the matter with mankind."[9] Here, surprisingly, we find a great consensus. Freud and Plato, Karl Marx and Ralph Nader, Martin Luther King Jr. and Gandhi and Jesus all agree with this—something is terribly wrong with us and cries out to be put right.

Being saved always involves being both saved *from* something and saved *for* something. We are saved for *shalom*—a flourishing life with God. What are we saved from?

Salvation as described in the Bible is about our being rescued from the whole chaotic mess that is our existence. There is no category of human need that God doesn't want to redeem. But it's the inner disorder of persons that the biblical writers say is our deepest problem. We are saved from brokenness, or death, or guilt, or wrath, or hell. We are saved from what we might otherwise become. We are saved—I know it sounds archaic—from evil.

Evil is a word that does not get used a lot in our culture. It sounds Victorian or melodramatic or nonscientific, or it's a punch line in a movie where a comical villain is called

Dr. Evil. A leading media personality had a conference on evil in Aspen, Colorado—the outcome of the meeting was that most of the participants did not believe that evil actually exists. (If evil is going to be considered, is Aspen really the right place for that conversation? Wouldn't Aleppo or Charlottesville be better?)

In the fall of 2017, the worst mass shooting in US history took place in Las Vegas, Nevada, and as periodically happens, we were faced with an event for which no other word seems adequate. *Evil* is to will the bad. Its definition is not confusing, though its origins and power are a mystery to us. To choose evil is to oppose God's Kingdom, whose watchword is *love*, to will the good. That's why in the prayer where Jesus says, "Your kingdom come; your will be done," he also says, "Deliver us from evil."

Evil is different from psychopathology or mental health problems, although of course evil is mentally unhealthy. Evil is the worst fate possible because it doesn't just happen *to* us. It happens *in* us.

Evil is simply this: to will the bad. Evil, when lodged in the human heart, goes by the biblical name *sin*.

We see most clearly what Jesus came to save us from in his name: "He will save his people *from their sins*" (Matthew 1:21, emphasis added). Dale Bruner notes the expression is so familiar we miss how surprising it would have been. Israel expected the Messiah to save them from the *consequences* of their sin— Roman occupation.[10] Similarly, in our day, salvation is often explained primarily in terms of escaping *punishment* for our sin. But the Bible says Jesus came to save us from *sin itself.* Being consumed by sin is more to be feared than being punished for it. William Faulkner wrote, "People to whom sin is just a matter of words, to them salvation is just words too."[11]

Any other force can only happen to you. Bullying, or sickness, or illness, or insult, or death. None of that can separate you from the love of God. Great ones among Jesus' followers have laughed at these.

Being overcome by evil is the ultimate tragedy that can befall a human being, and nothing else comes close. Suffering happens *to* you. Evil happens *in* you. It will claim your thoughts. It will twist your desires. It will corrupt your will. It will damn your soul.

Evil must be fought wherever it is found. But this is not a battle where Christians are the good guys and they fight the "bad guys." The battle is not in Las Vegas, Washington, or Hollywood. Aleksandr Solzhenitsyn once said, "If only there were evil people somewhere insidiously committing evil deeds, and it were necessary only to separate them from the rest of us and destroy them. But the line dividing good and evil cuts through the heart of every human being."[12]

Salvation doesn't mean simply being rescued from the consequences of our wrong choices. It doesn't mean being delivered into better circumstances. It means being changed. Salvation isn't primarily a matter of going to the good place. It's about becoming good people.

We need to be saved inwardly from our anger, despair, lust, greed, arrogance, and egotism. If our inner person is not transformed, our outer location won't matter much.

We often call this inner transformation—this forgiveness of sins—being "saved by grace." We have a tendency to view grace and forgiveness as being the same. But they are not synonymous. Grace is much bigger than forgiveness.

God was a gracious God before anyone ever sinned. Likewise, when Peter commanded people to "grow in grace" (see 2 Peter 3:18), he did not mean to "grow in the forgiveness of your sins."

According to Dallas Willard, grace is "God doing in us and for us what we could not do ourselves." We are meant to be forgiven by grace; we are also meant to *live* by grace. All of the gifts of energy and life we're given are gifts of grace. In our mistaken ideas, we often believe that only "sinners" need grace or that the only times we need grace are times of guilt. But as Dallas used to say, "Saints burn far more grace than sinners ever could. They burn it the way a jet burns rocket fuel." Salvation means that not only am I *forgiven* by grace, but I am also learning to *live* by grace. This is part of what makes boasting for any good that comes out of me as unthinkable as boasting for any sin forgiven in me—in either case, it is a gift of grace. Neal Plantinga wrote that this is what the grace of God is for—"not simply to balance a ledger, but to stimulate the spurts of growth in zeal, in enthusiasm for shalom, in good hard work, in sheer, delicious gratitude for the gift of life in all its pain and all its wonder."[13]

If grace is larger than forgiveness, then the assurance of my salvation is not simply believing that Jesus died for my sins to get me out of trouble and keep me out of the bad place. It is trusting in Jesus himself—that he was right about everything—and engaging in an interactive, grace-powered life with him beginning here and now. Isaiah 12:2 says,

> Surely God is my salvation;
>   I will trust and not be afraid.
> The LORD, the LORD himself, is my strength and
>   my defense;
> he has become my salvation.

My assurance is based on Jesus the *person*, not an arrangement I believe he has made on my behalf. My assurance is based on his character, his authority, his promise, and his will. It is based on a personal, participatory relationship with him where I grow to trust him more and more. That is how assurance of salvation and deliverance from fear works.

There's a wonderful old song: "Blessed assurance, Jesus is mine." The lyrics are not, "Blessed assurance—based on my compliance with the stipulations, they can't keep me out now." We trust the person, not the arrangement. As one writer puts it, "Christ doesn't save by going around handing out tickets to heaven. He saves by giving himself."[14]

SAVING SALVATION

Our understanding of salvation—what we are saved *for* and saved *from*—has a tremendous impact on how we live in the world. It's about being delivered from evil. If we view salvation wrongly as "making the cut," it violates the great commandment to love God because it makes God look unlovable and exclusive. It leads people to wonder, *Why doesn't God let more people into heaven?*

If we view salvation wrongly as "making the cut," we end up inadvertently violating the great commission. Jesus told us to make *disciples.* But if we essentially reduce salvation to getting into heaven, we are proclaiming a salvation that is disconnected from actually becoming disciples of Jesus. And the tragic result is millions of people who live needlessly untouched by the presence of God.

If we view salvation wrongly, people inside the church feel victimized by a bait-and-switch approach to the spiritual life. First, they're told that in order to become a Christian or to get "saved," they have to do absolutely nothing. Then, once they're in, they're told they're supposed to give to the poor, care for the sick and the elderly, and give their time, their money, and their possessions freely and without hesitation. Sometimes they're told they should do this out of gratitude for being forgiven, which creates the deadly illusion that obedience is something we do for God's sake rather than because it is the natural way of life for Jesus' disciples.

If we view salvation wrongly, it inevitably creates a warped sense of us versus them with those who haven't made the cut. It keeps people outside from coming in. It keeps people inside from changing.

The salvation that Jesus came to offer is bigger and grander and more vital than simply making the cut. It is the hope of the world. It is the reclamation of human life. It is the promise of meaning. It alone provides the security to live at peace each day, to face the past without guilt and the future without fear.

The reason we must understand Jesus' gospel aright is not just to be theologically correct. The reason is that the message we proclaim determines the kind of people we will produce.

If you proclaim, "The mall is at hand," you will tend to produce consumers.

If you proclaim, "TV is at hand," you will tend to produce spectators.

If you proclaim, "The revolution is at hand," you will tend to produce warriors.

If the church proclaims, "The gospel is how to get to heaven by doing nothing," it will tend to produce people who do nothing.

Much has been written in recent years about the problem of "consumer Christianity." But it is not often noted that the reason we have a tendency to produce consumer Christians is that we proclaim a gospel of consuming Jesus' merits to make sure we get to heaven when we die.

That's not what Jesus preached.

Jesus' gospel had a tendency to produce disciples. We'll look at what it means to be a disciple in the next chapter.

And trust me—it's Good News.

3

FOLLOW ME

Go and make disciples of all nations, baptizing
them in the name of the Father and of the
Son and of the Holy Spirit, and teaching them to
obey everything I have commanded you.

MATTHEW 28:19-20

When Louis Zamperini was thirty-two years old, he got saved.

Really saved.

It happened this way.

He had been a juvenile semidelinquent who discovered he could run like the wind and then became a famous Olympian. Shot down during World War II, he survived forty-seven days on a raft at sea with two men—one of whom died. He was reduced to skin and bones; ate an albatross, "eyeballs and all," like a chocolate sundae; and survived sharks, air attacks, and doldrums.

He prayed to God, *If you save me, I'll serve you forever.*

He was then picked up by the Japanese and locked in a POW camp that made the raft look like a cruise ship. Beaten, humiliated, tempted, and tortured, he prayed to be saved.

When the war ended, he was saved by the Allies and came home. And then came the worst suffering. Not from the outside. Not from a plane crash, or thirst, or sharks, or a sadistic prison guard. From himself.

He was tormented by his own fear and anger. He drank heavily, lied, lost money, raged, and bullied those around him. He tried to choke his wife. He drove everyone away from him. He even thought about ending his life.

Then his wife dragged him to a revival meeting led by a preacher named Billy Graham. At the end of the sermon, there was an invitation for lost lambs to come forward. Louis didn't want to, and he meant to leave the meeting, but he remembered his prayer—*If you save me, I'll serve you forever*—and his feet turned toward Graham.

He walked to the front of the meeting.

He got saved.

He went home and threw away the liquor and the girlie magazines that were part of his old life. He found the Bible given to him when he joined the air corps. "When he thought of his history, what resonated with him now was not all that he had suffered, but the divine love that he believed had intervened to save him. . . . His rage, his fear, his humiliation and helplessness, had fallen away. That morning, he believed, he was a new creation."[1]

Sixty years later, during the last year of his life, Louis came to speak at the church where I work. He had broken his leg two weeks before, and the doctor wouldn't let him fly, so he drove six hours with his son to come tell people he did not know about how he got saved more than sixty years ago and that there is hope for anyone.

This happened to a life.

It has happened to millions of lives.

It can happen to you.

269:3

Historians have long debated whether Abraham Lincoln was a Christian. Since his death in 1865, he has become a Rorschach test of sorts, upon which everybody projects their own beliefs. (I myself believe Lincoln was most certainly Presbyterian and probably Swedish.) In Michael Burkhimer's book on the subject, he notes that before you can decide about Lincoln, you must first confront "the essential question of what it means to be a Christian." He also notes that most writers and historians use three central beliefs as criteria. A Christian is someone who believes "that Jesus Christ was divine and part of a Trinity, that Christ died for the sins of the world, and that faith in this doctrine is necessary for one to gain salvation." While Burkhimer acknowledges this simplifies the matter, he notes, "It is a foundation almost all are familiar with."[2] What is striking is that the intention to actually follow Jesus by doing what he said—which was his fundamental call—has no part to play in this Christianity-defining "foundation almost all are familiar with."

Brad Wright, a sociologist at the University of Connecticut, notes that in social science research, a "Christian" is usually defined as someone who holds to certain doctrinal beliefs or who affiliates with a particular denomination or church.

Sometimes people's definitions of "Christian" are far more toxic. To paraphrase pastor Andy Stanley, many people would define "Christians" as moralistic, homophobic, anti-science, judgmental bigots who don't believe in dinosaurs but do believe they are the only ones going to heaven and secretly relish the idea that everyone else is going to hell.

Do you know what never defines the word *Christian*? The Bible. Literally. It never calls anyone to become a Christian, and it never records anyone becoming a Christian. Even Jesus never uses the word *Christian*. Jesus never says, "Here's how to become a Christian." Jesus never describes what a Christian is. Jesus himself wasn't even a Christian; he was Jewish. In fact, the word *Christian* is used only three times in the entire New Testament and then only because Jesus' followers were becoming too ethnically diverse to be regarded as a sect within Judaism. (World religions scholar Huston Smith notes that *Christian* simply meant "the Messiah-folk."[3]) Jesus didn't tell his friends, "Go into all the world and make *Christians*." But he *did* tell them to go into the world and make disciples.

In fact, the Bible uses the word *disciple* 269 times. As Dallas Willard writes, "The New Testament is a book about disciples, by disciples, and for disciples."[4]

How is a disciple different from a Christian? Are disciples a subcategory of overachievers? Are they the dean's list? Is discipleship optional, like whitewall tires? Maybe the bar is higher. Maybe it's only disciples who will get into heaven, while so-called Christians will be shut out—the lukewarm ones God will spew out of his mouth.

For many people—inside the church and out—Christians are thought of as people who believe the gospel of the minimum entrance requirements, who are saved because they believe the right things, which means they will be allowed into heaven when they die.

The gospel of the minimum entrance requirements is what Dietrich Bonhoeffer calls "cheap grace":

> The upshot of [cheap grace] is that my only duty as a Christian is to leave the world for an hour or so on a Sunday morning and go to church to be assured that my sins are all forgiven. I need no longer try to follow Christ, for cheap grace, the bitterest foe of discipleship, which true discipleship must loathe and detest, has freed me from that."[5]

But we now know that Jesus never said, "Believe the right things about me, and I'll let you into heaven after you die." His news was something far grander, more cosmic, more life-changing, more costly, more compelling, and more humbling than that.

To the contrary, Jesus' Good News is that eternal life—life *with* God and *for* God, life *under* God's care and life *by* God's power—is available now. If you want that life, the logical step is to become a disciple—a student, an apprentice, a follower—of Jesus.

Simply put, discipleship is the means by which we learn to live the life that Jesus offers. Christianity was never intended to produce Christians. Just disciples.

ARE YOU AN INNIE OR AN OUTIE?

Jesus' disciples have two great commandments: love God with all their hearts, and love the people in their lives the way they love themselves. Jesus said this is how his identity and mission would be verified—by the existence of a community of irrationally loving disciples.[6]

Those of us who call ourselves "Christians," who have defined ourselves by affirming right beliefs, often wrestle with having a reputation for exclusivity and judgmentalism, a spirit of us versus them, and a difficulty in embracing the "other."

However, one of the most striking aspects of Jesus' approach to people was the way he treated those who were thought to be in the "out" group. Yale theologian Miroslav Volf writes that one of the greatest differences between Jesus and the establishment religious leaders of his time was that they regarded exclusion of the moral or religious "other" as a virtue, whereas Jesus regarded such exclusion as sin. He was strangely welcoming to people normally shunned. His followers learned, often slowly and painfully, to follow in this way.

So how does one define a follower of Jesus? Here's one way of thinking about it that I've found helpful. An old teacher of mine named Paul Hiebert wrote an article that defined two different ways of sorting objects as either in or out.[7]

One way is by what's called a "bounded set." With bounded sets, the way you determine whether an object is in or out is by carefully defining the boundary. For instance, you could determine whether something is a triangle by saying that it must meet the minimum requirements of being a geometric shape that has exactly three distinct sides and three distinct angles. Membership in a bounded set is *clear*—something is either in or out. Membership in a bounded set is *static*. A circle will never be a triangle. It cannot become more triangle-y. And a triangle cannot become square-ish. The object either satisfies the criteria or it doesn't.

Another kind of set is called a "centered set." Here, objects in the set are defined by their orientation to the center. Membership in the set is dynamic, not static. What matters is movement.

Take, for example, the set "bald people." The absolute center—the exemplar—is Mr. Clean, the completely hair-free cartoon detergent spokesman. Someone totally *outside* this group would be the profusely haired Albert Einstein. Now, a baby may be born bald—and so is in the group—but she's growing hair, so she's on her way out. On the other hand, a twenty-year-old may have a full head of hair, but it's beginning to recede, so he's on his way in. What's the minimum number of hairs required to be part of the group? Only God—who has numbered the hairs on your head—knows for sure.

A centered set is neither subjective nor vague. It is simply defined in relation to the center as opposed to the boundary.

If we think of Christianity as a bounded set, we will focus on the boundary. We will want to define what the necessary and sufficient conditions are for being in. Maybe it's that someone checked "Christian" as their preferred religion on a survey, or prayed the sinner's prayer, or professed a belief that Jesus is divine. Regardless, membership in the group is static. You either are a member or you aren't, and your status is defined solely by the minimum requirements determined by some outside authority—usually the church or other Christians.

However, the New Testament presents a community of disciples that looks much more like a centered set than a bounded set. The center is Jesus. He defines and incarnates life in the Kingdom of God and makes it available to others. This life is a call to love God with all that you are and to love your neighbor as yourself.

Some people—like certain religious leaders—worked hard to demonstrate that they were in. They knew the Scriptures and paid particular attention to things like Sabbath-keeping, circumcision, and dietary laws. Yet they refused to orient themselves toward Jesus and his kind of agape love. Jesus says they're actually *outside* his Kingdom.

Other people, like the sinful woman in Luke 7 or Zacchaeus the tax collector, look a million miles outside the people of God. Yet when they turn toward Jesus, he says things like "Her many sins have been forgiven" (Luke 7:47) and "Today salvation has come to this house" (Luke 19:9).

In fact, what got Jesus into more trouble than anything else is that he often warned people who were sure they were insiders that they were in danger of being outside, and he treated people everyone knew were outsiders as though they might actually be in. Samaritans, lepers, centurions, Canaanite women, divorcées, and more were treated this way.

The Scripture writers revel in this sort of thing. When Rahab is identified in the book of Joshua, she is described as "a prostitute named Rahab." When she's affirmed in Hebrews as a heroic character, she's called "the prostitute Rahab." When she's cited as an example of good works in James, she's called "Rahab the prostitute."[8]

Really? Is there no other adjective available? Rahab the redhead, or the southpaw, or the vegetarian? Clearly, Rahab stands as an example of someone who appears *not* to fall within the established boundary markers, yet she is part of what God is doing.

If Christianity is a bounded set, then we will want to be very clear about what the necessary and sufficient conditions are to get people inside. Our goal will be to get people to cross the boundary from outside to inside. Once they're in, any further progress is optional. We can turn our attention to others who we believe have not yet crossed the boundary. If Christianity is a bounded set, we will tend to focus on those issues that differentiate who is in and who is out, rather than those issues that were central to Jesus' primary concern. We will find ourselves, for example, placing more weight on attitudes about sexual behaviors than about helping the poor—not because Jesus said that sexuality was more important than poverty but because there's a clearer boundary. Our culture generally affirms concern for the poor but often differs with the church about sexual morality. We will become more concerned with what attitudes and behavior separate us from those outside than about what concerns were most central to Jesus.

However, if following Jesus is about the center, then we will want to constantly orient ourselves toward God and his will and his love. We will want to be ever moving toward it. We will want to invite and help other people to be ever moving toward it. What matters is the orientation and posture of our lives. We are not worried about who is us and who is them. We know that God knows, and that is enough for us. We trust him to do right by each person, including those we love most.

This is why having a centered approach to Jesus is so helpful. It reminds us that following Jesus is not a static religious identity but a dynamic calling that constantly invigorates and challenges us.

Someone once asked cellist Pablo Casals—since he was in his eighties and was the best cellist in the world—why he kept practicing for hours every day. He responded, "Because I think I'm getting better."

Paul wrote, "Not that I have already obtained all this, or have already been made perfect. . . . But one thing I do: Forgetting what is behind and straining toward what is ahead, I press on toward the goal to win the prize for which God has called me heavenward in Christ Jesus" (Philippians 3:12-14). Paul, you're already "in"—why do you keep pressing on?

"Because I think I'm getting better."

In the same letter Paul writes, "Continue to work out your salvation with fear and trembling, for it is God who works in you to will and to act according to his good purpose" (Philippians 2:12-13). Biblical salvation is *so much more* than having satisfied the minimum requirements. It is the grace-powered redemption of our thoughts and desires and will and action into cosmic meaning and divine love that leads us ever onward and upward.

It's the dynamic rather than static nature of life that led C. S. Lewis to write, "The world does not consist of 100 percent Christians and 100 percent non-Christians. There are people (a great many of them) who are slowly ceasing to be Christians but who still call themselves by that name: some of them are clergymen. There are other people who are slowly becoming Christians though they do not yet call themselves so. . . . It is some use comparing cats and dogs . . . in the mass, because there one knows definitely which is which. Also, an animal does not turn (either slowly or suddenly) from a dog into a cat."[9]

But human beings *are* in the process of "turning into" something—something wonderful or something wicked—all the time. From God's perspective, of course, there is no ambiguity about human destiny. He promises human beings that we can be accepted and justified and sealed in the Spirit to encourage all who would follow Jesus that this is not ultimately a human enterprise.

That's why, while a centered-set approach may help us understand how we define *discipleship*, it remains true that boundaries are indispensable for life—including spiritual life. Divinity schools may need to define the doctrinal boundaries for someone to serve on a faculty. Parents need to be able to say certain behaviors are out of bounds for their children. Churches need to do the same for members. Paul does this when he warns the church in Corinth about tolerating sexual immorality (see 1 Corinthians 5). And perhaps the most famous warnings in religious literature are given by Jesus himself about religious hypocrisy in Matthew 23 ("Woe to you, teachers of the law . . .").

In fact, it is precisely because Jesus is so clear about the center ("Love God with all your heart," "love your neighbor as yourself") that he is able to be clear about his warnings when someone is violating love. There is nothing "soft" or ambiguous about his warnings. To the contrary, they're part of what got him killed. But these warnings did not focus on what were the "boundary marker" issues of his day—circumcision, dietary laws, or Sabbath-keeping. The people he warned were precisely those who prided themselves on being way inside the boundaries while in fact their spiritual trajectory was away from the Kingdom. ("You blind guides! You strain out a gnat but swallow a camel"—Matthew 23:24.)

When people define "Christian" in terms of having satisfied the minimum entrance requirements for getting into heaven, it always leads to "where to set the bar" debates. Some people set a high bar, saying that only a few radically obedient followers will get into heaven. People who take such a position are considered either champions of radical commitment or exclusionary or legalistic, depending on whether you agree with them.

Others will set a low bar for getting into heaven. They are considered either champions of grace or lax about sin or soft on doctrine, depending on whether you agree with them.

Jesus is radically gracious in his desire to accept and love. He is radically severe in his warnings about sin and God's judgment. He is radically silent about the minimum amount that a "borderline" person needs to believe or do to get into heaven when they die.

The "bar" Jesus sets for discipleship is not arbitrary. It is not, in that sense, a low bar or a high bar. The bar for pursuing sobriety in Alcoholics Anonymous or for becoming a great cellist or an excellent parent is set by reality. Someone who genuinely wants it above all else will do whatever it takes and consider it a bargain. So it is with disciples who want to live in the Kingdom of God. They will follow Jesus. Their life is centered around him.

That is why, when it comes to the question of who is in with God and who is out, Jesus and the New Testament consistently focus on the center, not on the boundaries.

There is an old tradition on large Australian ranches located on often-dry land that there are two ways of keeping cattle on the ranch. One is to build a fence; the other is to dig a well. What a gift it might be to a world that has become increasingly polarized and politicized if the church would be utterly committed to Jesus as our center. No fences to keep others out, just the life-giving water of Jesus, drawing people ever closer to his presence.

WELCOME TO THE INNER CIRCLE

Jesus may not have had anything to say about what a Christian is, but he was very clear about what a disciple is: "Whoever wants to be my disciple must deny themselves and take up their cross daily and follow me" (Luke 9:23).

Another way to say it is the way Dallas Willard put it: "A disciple is someone whose ultimate goal is to live their life the way Jesus would live if he were me."

That's where *apprentice* is such a helpful word. An apprentice is someone who commits themselves to be with a master craftsman and to learn from them how to master the craft. The word for *disciple* in the New Testament was often used for trade apprenticeship. It's not a special church word for the spiritual elite. Anyone can do it. It's not about the skill of the apprentice; it's about the power of the Master.

Simon Sinek gave a famous TED talk where he described what he calls "the golden circle."[10] Any company, movement, or cause will have three concentric circles. The outer circle is the "what"—here's what we make or do. Inside that is a smaller circle, the "how"—here's how we do it.

As a general rule, in the life of organizations, everybody will know the "what." And most people will know the "how." But very few will know what's in the third circle, the innermost circle—the golden circle. That circle contains the "why."

The church's "what" is to make disciples, or apprentices. The "how" is by learning to be with Jesus and by learning from Jesus how to live like Jesus. We do this through spiritual practices, through experiences like suffering, and through the guidance of the Holy Spirit.

That leads to the "why." Dallas Willard defines the "why" like this: "There is no problem in human life that apprenticeship to Jesus cannot solve."

You name the problem—greed, fear, racism, injustice, divorce, sexual assault, neglect, pollution, suffering, addiction, rejection, bitterness, violence, apathy, grief, war, death.

Human problems will not be solved by human means.

Human problems will not be solved by human nature.

Human nature is our biggest problem.

There are many problems technology will never solve.

There are many problems education will never solve.

There are many problems money will never solve.

There are many problems religion will never solve.

But there is no problem in human life that apprenticeship to Jesus cannot solve. That includes the forgiveness of our sins and the promise of life with God forever after death, but it also includes every other part of our existence, starting with here and now.

Jesus' gospel is the offer of life as an apprentice of Jesus, by grace, through faith, in this world and the world to come. It is the greatest invitation ever given to human beings. Because there is no problem in human life that apprenticeship to Jesus cannot solve.

This is why Dietrich Bonhoeffer wrote, "Grace and discipleship are inseparable" (although in our day, we've tried to make them separable!). "Happy are they who know that discipleship simply means the life which springs from grace, and that grace simply means discipleship."[11]

Many people think that the mission of the church is to make more Christians. After all, there are lots of other religions around, as well as agnostics and atheists—we don't want them to win; we want *us* to win.

But Jesus did not instruct his church to create more Christians. He instructed them to make apprentices. Because there is no problem in life that apprenticeship to Jesus cannot solve.

It's time to see what apprenticeship to Jesus looks like.

PART 2

WALKING WITH JESUS

THE GREAT JOURNEY

There are only two or three human stories,
and they go on repeating themselves as fiercely
as if they had never happened before.

WILLA CATHER

One of the stories that "go on repeating themselves"—perhaps the Great Story—is the story of the journey. From *The Odyssey* to *The Pilgrim's Progress* to *The Divine Comedy* to *The Wizard of Oz* to *The Lord of the Rings*, an ordinary character leaves home to enter a strange, unknown world. The character faces dangers, toils, and snares; they die and are reborn; they are delivered; they are saved; they come home. This story, retold a thousand times, never grows old because it is our story.

Your soul is on a journey to God.

The Bible is a book of such journeys. Abraham leaves home to go to a place that God will show him. Joseph journeys down to Egypt; hundreds of years later Moses journeys from Egypt back home. Israel knows the strange, sad journey of exile. The center of the story is the great journey of the one to whom all heroes point: Jesus journeys from heaven to earth; he sets his face toward Jerusalem; he journeys to the cross, and hell itself, and then back to life and heaven, only now with the gift of salvation to give to all who desire it.

Salvation is a journey to God.

So it is time to turn from thinking about salvation to actually living it. Paul said, "Work out your salvation with fear and trembling, for it is God who works in you to will and to act in order to fulfill his good purpose" (Philippians 2:12-13). We don't work *for* our salvation, but we do work *out* our salvation.

If we think of salvation as acquiring the right afterlife by affirming correct doctrine, it becomes a static and stagnant thing. It leads to tremendous frustration that people inside the church and out often have with reality—we talk about wonderful spiritual realities but do not know how to pursue them. We are only window shopping.

In *The Pilgrim's Progress*, Christian's journey begins at the Wicket-gate. "Here is a poor burdened sinner," he says, fleeing from destruction on his way to Mount Zion. It is the narrow gate Jesus calls all his followers to enter. Dallas Willard writes, "The narrow gate is not, as so often assumed, doctrinal correctness. The narrow gate is obedience—and the confidence in Jesus necessary to it. . . . The broad gate, by contrast, is simply doing whatever I want to do."[1]

I sometimes wonder, if *The Pilgrim's Progress* had been

written in our day, it might have been called *The Pilgrim's Recess* instead. The dangerous, confusing, exhilarating journey of actually following Jesus is thought to be optional as long as you've asked for forgiveness based on correct doctrine.

The journey of a soul toward God begins with the intention to follow Jesus, made concrete in the *decision* to seek to obey him from moment to moment. A decision cuts us off from alternatives. We speak of the road to hell being paved with good *intentions* but not with good *decisions*.

We leave on our journey, we enter the Wicket-gate, when we intend to obey Jesus in all things, knowing that we can only begin the effort through the power of him who is "at work . . . to will and to act" in us. This is why his signature call is not "arrange to get justified" but simply "follow me."

Obedience to Jesus in all things *is* the journey, but as we will see, obedience is a far more creative, proactive, grace-powered, intelligent way of life than is normally thought in our day.

The gospel is sometimes expressed along these lines: "The bad news is you're a worse sinner than you thought; the good news is you're more loved than you know." Imagine an alcoholic who received that "gospel." It has good news but not enough of it. An alcoholic needs to be loved, but she also needs to be saved from her alcoholism.

In the Twelve Steps, a constant refrain is a call to action. One chapter that lays out the steps is simply called "Into Action." It ends with these words: "But this is not all. There is action and more action. 'Faith without works is dead.'"[2]

We need action because to be human is to act. We are constantly thinking and seeing and choosing and feeling. It is in our ordinary, everyday actions that salvation gets worked out. Martin Luther spoke about this with gusto: "Oh, faith is a living, busy, active, mighty thing, so that it is impossible for it not to be constantly doing what is good. Likewise, faith does not ask if good works are to be done, but before one can ask, faith has already done them and is constantly active. Whoever does not perform such good works is a faithless man."[3]

The action that we need is not a devotional to-do list to add on to an already exhausting way of life. It is more the transformation of the actions we are constantly engaged in. Not tiring but rejuvenating. Not draining but refilling.

We need a path to follow. A journey without a path or direction is called being lost.

So in the rest of this book, it's time for action as we pursue the soul's journey together. For many centuries, the best way of describing that journey has involved certain stages that we're going to look at together. They are not particularly linear; we can go back and forth between them. But they are dynamics that describe the way God works in our lives.

- *Awakening:* I become aware of God's extraordinary presence in my ordinary days. I wake up to gratitude and awe and responsibility. Awareness of God interrupts my tendency to live in what author Linda Stone has called "Continuous Partial Attention," never being fully present to my life.[4] The journey begins.

- *Purgation:* I begin to see all the ways I respond to life and people that keep God at arm's length. I confess my character defects. I ask God to remove them. I engage in practices that can help free me from them. As time passes, I come to see them even more clearly.
- *Illumination:* I begin to change at the level of my automatic perceptions and beliefs. My "mental map" of how things are begins to look more like Jesus' mental map. I live in the peace and joy of safety in his hand.
- *Union:* I begin to experience the life that Jesus described when he said, "Abide in me, and I will abide in you" (see John 15:4). His presence becomes a reality and not just an idea.[5]

There are potential misunderstandings in talking about the spiritual life involving stages. One misunderstanding is that we'll think of them as concrete phases that we pass through and are forever done with, like infancy or adolescence. But the spiritual life is not that way. It's more like playing Monopoly, where I go around the board many times; both Jail and Boardwalk are familiar to me. I may be relatively purged of sin in one area yet deeply wrestling with sin in another. Thomas Merton wrote that when it comes to the spiritual life, we are always beginners.[6] New Testament scholar Dale Bruner put it more graphically: "I am not really born again; I'm in about my second trimester."[7]

Furthermore, regression is always possible. In fact, it's particularly true in the realm of the spirit that any time we think we have attained a great deal, we are actually more vulnerable to pride and self-sufficiency. There's an old Irish proverb: "The higher we climb, the higher the devil climbs."[8]

Talking about stages can also mask our daily, desperate need for God. One of the principles in Alcoholics Anonymous is that we can never rest on our spiritual laurels. Instead, what we have is a "daily reprieve" from the mess we would make apart from surrender and grace. It is the Prodigal Son's elder brother, who thought he was so good and obedient, who was actually the most lost child in Jesus' story. We are never done developing. This is why St. Francis said to his friends at the end of his earthly life, "Let us begin now, because so far we have done nothing."[9]

The goal of the spiritual life is not to "get through" the stages. It is always, in any moment—even in this one—to take the next small step on the great journey to God.

Each morning I ask God to awaken me to his presence and the meaning of my life. Each day I recognize more baggage that I will have to jettison if I am to stay on the path. Moments of confusion will give way to insight as God illumines my way. In moments of deepest aloneness I will come to know that I am never alone.

In the last few chapters we've looked at why this journey is necessary. For the next several chapters we'll look at how Jesus led his first students on this journey and how we can go with them.

The good news is that we do not journey alone. In *The Pilgrim's Progress*, Christian is constantly making the wrong choice. He falls into the Slough of Despond, listens to Mr. Worldly Wiseman, leaves the highway, and gets trapped in Doubting-castle. He is a remedial pilgrim. But heaven is patient. Every other page, it's "Recalculating route. When possible, make a U-turn." Pilgrim gets this one thing right: he stays on the journey. "I press on to take hold of that for which Christ Jesus took hold of me" (Philippians 3:12).

"We must, in fact, do nothing less than engage in a radical rethinking of the Christian conception of salvation."[10] What does it mean to be saved? We have come to the Wicket-gate. Let's follow Jesus on the road of discipleship.

4

AWAKENING
Seeing God Everywhere

Peter and his companions were very sleepy, but when they
became fully awake, they saw his glory.

LUKE 9:32

Frederick Buechner wrote, "As far as I know, there has never
been an age that has not produced fairy tales."[1] He says the reason fairy tales are universal is that they teach us what we most
need to know about life.

They tell us that things are often not what they seem—the
ugly frog is really a prince, the lovely stepmother is in fact a
witch.

They tell us that there is another world that this world points
to. That world is not so far away, and we are not in control of it.

They tell us that stepping into a wardrobe or falling down a
rabbit hole or rubbing a lamp suddenly introduces a new reality.
What was ordinary is suddenly the vehicle of the extraordinary.

Often the problem in fairy tales is that because of a curse or a spell, someone has fallen into a death sleep from which they are powerless to awake. Maybe it's the bite of a poison apple or the prick of a spinning wheel or a nap that lasts twenty years.

These stories endure because they're our story. We find ourselves blind to urgent matters as if we have been spellbound. But sometimes we do awaken from our enchanted sleep. Bill W. awakens one day to the reality that he's a hopeless addict and founds Alcoholics Anonymous. Scarlett O'Hara awakens to the fact that she's really in love with Rhett Butler and not Ashley Wilkes. Ebenezer Scrooge awakens to the pain of his miserly past and the possibility of a generous future. We might awaken to our failure as parents, or our workaholism, or the reality that we've been living in fear or anger. We might awaken to a new passion for music or surfing, or to a calling to fight racism or poverty.

Or we might awaken to God.

This is what happens in the Bible. A fugitive from Egypt named Moses sees a bush he's passed a hundred times before, but this time it's on fire. He turns aside and hears the voice of God.

The story of the Bible is like a fairy tale because it points us to another, deeper reality, only the story of the Bible is true. It actually happened.

Our journey toward God begins with awakening. Robert Mulholland writes that we awaken toward two primary realities: we encounter the true God in our world, and we encounter the truth about ourselves as we really are. Until this happens, we are dead to the possibilities of spiritual life. With awakening, he writes, come two primary emotions: comfort and threat. Comfort because God is good and life with him means "our universe is a perfectly safe place for us to be."[3] Threat because there is much in us that is not good and will have to be changed if we are to live with God. And change will mean pain.

Without such awakenings, the energy and power of spiritual life recedes. Faith becomes secondhand, routine. William James wrote about the experience of awakening happening "in individuals for whom religion exists not as *a dull habit*, but as *an acute fever*."[4]

No one was ever saved from alcoholism, or moved to give away their possessions, or inspired to go to jail for civil rights by a dull habit.

Harvard's Bill Leonard writes of a group of seminarians listening to the conversion story of a young, uneducated Appalachian man named Adam, a meth-cooking, hard-drinking, fast-driving "screw-up." He crashed a pickup truck, but when he and his friends were spared what should have been death, he recognized the grace of God and surrendered his life. His Free Will Baptist mother shouted praises for days. He began to preach in the county jail where he would have ended up had not the judge, like Jesus, given him a second chance. He said he "got saved hard." Leonard writes that Adam's spiritual awakening was so powerful that "'even the Presbyterian students' were reduced to tears."[5]

Adam's story is not mine, and attempts to manufacture dramatic religious experiences or embellish spiritual stories can do great damage. But no one who has met Jesus goes away with a dull habit.

From earliest times, teachers have struggled to awaken their students. An ancient Sumerian riddle asked, "Whoever enters it has closed eyes; whoever departs from it has eyes that are wide open. What is it?" The answer is a school. Closed eyes are a picture of ignorance and prejudice and even the refusal to know. Of course, James Crenshaw writes that in order to open their students' eyes, ancient Sumerian teachers "beat them vigorously."[6]

In ancient Israel, students were introduced to three paths of knowledge: observation of the world, report of the learning of others, and direct encounter with the Transcendent One.

It is this last path that we take now.

A MOUNTAINTOP EXPERIENCE

Imagine standing on a mountain called Mount Tabor.

Very often in the Bible people have encounters with God on mountains. The Bible is, among other things, a book about mountains. They are mentioned hundreds of times. Moses meets the divine presence at a burning bush on what is called "the mountain of God" (Exodus 3:1). It was Mount Sinai where God made his covenant with people and where the people chose to keep God "at a distance" (20:18, 21) It was on a mountain that Elijah heard the still, small voice of God.

Mountains especially mark the life of Jesus. It was on a high mountain that he renounced the temptation to receive all the kingdoms of the world. It was on a mountain that he chose his disciples. The most famous talk in human history is the Sermon on the Mount. The most famous and influential death in history was on a hill called Mount Calvary, where humanity witnessed the extent of God's love. The most famous and influential mission in history—to make disciples who will obey Jesus in everything—was given by Jesus to his disciples at "the mountain where [he] had told them to go" (Matthew 28:16).

A mountain is where heaven and earth come closest together. A mountain is where we go to see the earth around us from a new perspective. On a mountain we are elevated above our normal way of seeing. Obstacles that normally loom large are seen as much smaller than we thought. From a mountain we are able to see parts of the world that were not visible to us from below. On a mountain we receive the gift of vision.

We're told that one day, "Jesus went up on a mountainside and called to him those he wanted, and they came to him. He appointed twelve—designating them apostles—that they might *be with him*" (Mark 3:13-14, emphasis added). The idea wasn't just that they would occupy the same space. To be with Jesus meant they would become his intimate friends. They would open their hearts up to him; they would learn from him; they would be transparent with him; they would enjoy and admire him and then trust him, be undone and then remade by him.

Jesus called them on a mountain because a calling is a

mountaintop experience. The disciples awoke to a purpose and identity that they did not have the day before. Their primary calling was simply to be with Jesus. And it happened as he said it would. After Jesus left the earth, two of his friends got in trouble with the religious leaders. "When they saw the courage of Peter and John and realized that they were unschooled, ordinary men, they were astonished and they took note that these men *had been with Jesus*" (Acts 4:13, emphasis added).

Better to be unschooled and ordinary *with* Jesus than schooled and extraordinary *without* Jesus.

A mountain is the place of awakening to a reality that we often can't see in the valley. Above all, it is awakening to the gospel of Jesus—the availability of life in the presence and power and grace and care of God *now*.

In his book *A Secular Age*, Charles Taylor explores why faith is so hard, particularly for those in the West. He notes that five hundred years ago it was hard for people *not* to believe in God, but today all of us—even believers—live in a valley of doubt. We live in what he calls an "immanent frame," a boxed-in way of viewing the world that simply assumes material reality is all that exists.[7] According to this view, we live in a terrarium—a very large, complex cosmic terrarium with a lid on it. However, we long for what he calls "fullness" of life—real moral goodness, ennobling beauty, truly responsible lives.[8] But we are no longer confident in a transcendent spiritual and moral realm that makes all that real.

So we, too, need a mountain.

There is another world. Things are not what they seem. O sleeper, awake.

That's why the story of what is called the Transfiguration of Jesus plays such a prominent role in the New Testament. It is our journey through the wardrobe and down the rabbit hole and up the beanstalk, our glimpse of the other world, that enables us to live wide awake in this one.

It begins this way:

> After six days Jesus took with him Peter, James and John the brother of James, and led them up a high mountain by themselves. There he was transfigured before them. His face shone like the sun, and his clothes became as white as the light. Just then there appeared before them Moses and Elijah, talking with Jesus.
>
> MATTHEW 17:1-3

The lid is off the terrarium.

The likely reason for Matthew telling us the time frame is that in the Bible six days is often the number of days needed to prepare a transcendent experience.

Creation happened in six days—on the seventh day God invited people into the experience of Sabbath.

For six days the glory of God covered Mount Sinai in a

cloud; on the seventh day God called to Moses to enter into the cloud.

Here in Matthew, six days have passed since Peter confessed at Caesarea Philippi that Jesus is the Christ, the Son of the living God (see 16:16). The call to the mountaintop does not come on our timetable. It comes at the right time, not our time. The sixth day, not the first day.

Then he invites Peter, James, and John to an experience. He wants to share an experience with them that will create a new level of knowing and intimacy in their relationship.

They could have begged off. They could have said they had so much disciple work to do *for* Jesus that they didn't have time to be *with* Jesus.

Peter, James, and John got a lot wrong, but they got this right: when Jesus called them to come to him on the mountain, they said yes.

It's worth pausing to think about the role of experience in awakening to God.

Dallas Willard said that persons are made up of experiences. We don't consist merely or even primarily of cells and tissue; our real lives are a series of experiences.

That's why we treasure a sunset or a great meal or a view from a mountain. People often use their cell phones to take pictures of themselves, which significantly enough we call "selfies." But we don't take selfies at random. We don't wake up and say, "Hey—I think I'll take a selfie today." We do it before the ocean, or beside a waterfall, or at a concert, or with a friend.

C. S. Lewis writes that our deepest experiences awaken a desire in us that we can hardly find a name for, a desire the material world cannot satisfy—a desire for love or beauty or meaning, which the Bible calls "glory." Our experiences awaken this desire, but

> they are not the thing itself; they are only the scent of a flower we have not found, the echo of a tune we have not heard, news from a country we have never yet visited. Do you think I am trying to weave a spell? Perhaps I am; but remember your fairy tales. Spells are used for breaking enchantments as well as for inducing them. And you and I have need of the strongest spell that can be found to wake us from the evil enchantment of worldliness which has been laid upon us for nearly a hundred years. . . . We remain conscious of a desire which no natural happiness will satisfy.[9]

Intimacy is shared experience. That's why inviting someone to watch a movie or to get a cup of coffee or even to take a walk is such a vulnerable thing. When you invite someone to share an experience, you're inviting them into a little step of intimacy. By inviting Peter, James, and John up the mountain, Jesus was inviting them into intimacy.

Spiritual awakening begins with an experience of God, when we become aware of his presence. It may come through beauty—a walk in a forest or a piece of music. It may come through pain—the loss of a job, the end of a marriage, a dire diagnosis. It may come through change—falling in love, the birth of a baby. It may come through the reading of Scripture, as it did for Augustine or for John Wesley, whose "heart was strangely warmed." It might happen in a church, as it did for Anne Lamott, who against her will found love and sobriety and Jesus and got baptized and said, "I swear, it was an accident!"[10] It might happen in prison, as it did for Chuck Colson. It might be quite undramatic.

But it happens. We become aware of the reality of the unseen. Awakening is, in a loaded phrase quoted by Evelyn Underhill, "primarily an unselfing."[11] The first time I awaken, at birth, it is to my own little world where my desires and survival are the center. But on the mountain I awaken to a much larger world. My ego is decentered. I am open to intimacy with God.

A GLOWING REALITY

Peter, James, and John look at Jesus. He is transfigured.

I try to imagine this.

The great Old Testament blessing was "the LORD make his face shine upon you" (Numbers 6:25). They see it.

The promise of Revelation is that the saints will wear white linen, which stands for moral beauty. They see it.

There was a deep connection in the ancient world between transcendent glory and shining light. Even in our day, when a grandparent looks at a grandchild, we say their face *beams*. When people describe a bride on her wedding day, what's the most common adjective? She looks *radiant*. (There is no word to describe the groom. No one cares.)

When Moses came down from Mount Sinai, "he was not aware that his face was radiant because he had spoken with the LORD. When Aaron and all the Israelites saw Moses, his face was radiant, and they were afraid to come near him" (Exodus 34:29-30).

The psalmist said, "Those who look to him are radiant; their faces are never covered with shame" (Psalm 34:5).

Light is energy. Light is beauty. But with Jesus, this experience reaches a new height. Moses saw the shekinah glory of God and reflected it the way the moon reflects the light of the sun. Jesus *radiated* it. His light wasn't a reflection; he was the source. John—who was on this mountain with Jesus—would say about him later, "In him was life, and that life was the light of all mankind" (John 1:4).

Jesus has the most recognizable face in the world. In pictures and movies he has long brown hair, a well-trimmed beard, and great teeth; he speaks with a British accent; and his robe has a blue sash like Miss America.

The New Testament writers never describe what Jesus looks like. His physical appearance is unimportant to them. There is an Old Testament passage about a suffering servant that they applied to Jesus: "He had no beauty or majesty to attract us to him, nothing in his appearance that we should desire him" (Isaiah 53:2). Based partly on this, early Christian thinkers like Tertullian and Justin Martyr believed Jesus to be physically unattractive. A second-century figure named Celcius described Jesus as "ugly and small."

Some scholars believe it's possible there was something about Jesus' physical appearance that looked deformed or unhealthy or that needed fixing. It is possible that in a world that often worships beauty rather than God, Jesus knew what it was to be not beautiful. It is possible that in his very physical appearance, he was saying to the world, "Be careful about judging things and people too quickly. If you see only what's on the surface, you will be deceived. If you want to find true beauty, you have to look for it."

There is another world. It's not far away. Things are not what they seem. In the strange world of the Kingdom of God, the frog turns out to be a prince; the ugly duckling is a beautiful swan; the crucified carpenter is the King of kings and the Lord of lords.

Jesus' gospel is that in him the Kingdom of God has become available on earth. The presence of this spiritual reality is manifested repeatedly in the Old Testament—through a rainbow; a burning bush; a still, small voice; handwriting on the wall; a shining cloud.

Now in the Transfiguration comes its ultimate expression.

The disciples are allowed for a moment to see what Jesus already knew—that we live in a God-bathed, God-permeated world. Dallas Willard writes, "It is a world that is inconceivably beautiful and good because of God and because God is always in it. It is a world in which God is continually at play and over which he constantly rejoices. Until our thoughts of God have found every visible thing and event glorious with his presence, the word of Jesus has not yet fully seized us."[12] *wow*

The Transfiguration story goes on: "Peter and his companions were very sleepy, but when they became fully awake, they saw his glory" (Luke 9:32).

"When they became fully awake . . ."

Waking is a great mystery to us. We fall asleep—and do not know how it happens. We wake up—and that is mystery as well. When we sleep, we are dead to the world. The world around us is still there, but we are not aware of it and cannot engage with it. When we awaken, what we awaken to is the world around us.

I have a friend who had to take an international flight and wanted to sleep. Someone gave him the sedative Ambien, but he was skeptical. He took one pill—nothing happened. He took a second—still nothing. He took a third pill and this time washed it down with a glass of wine.

When he woke up, he was sitting in a strange terminal, in a wheelchair, with drool on his shirt. He had slept so hard, the flight attendants couldn't wake him up when the plane landed, so they just wheeled him out of the plane and left him at the gate.

Sin is like spiritual Ambien, and because of sin, many of us are like my friend, so asleep to the reality of God around us that it seems impossible we should ever wake up. Yet with God, nothing is impossible.

It is important to understand that awakening is a gift and not an achievement. This is true each morning (though if you're not a morning person, it may not feel like it). Sleep happens to us, and wakefulness is given to us in the morning. The one person in all the world that you cannot wake up is yourself.

English poet Francis Thompson wrote a haunting poem called "The Hound of Heaven" that deeply moved Christian thinkers like G. K. Chesterton and J. R. R. Tolkien and John Stott. It's a picture of God pursuing human beings, relentless as a hound, for the purpose of love and redemption. It's a picture of how his desire to pursue us is stronger than our intent to flee:

> *I fled Him, down the nights and down the days;*
> *I fled Him, down the arches of the years;*
> *I fled Him, down the labyrinthine ways*
> *Of my own mind; and in the mist of tears*
> *I hid from Him, and under running laughter.*

God pursues us though we hide from him in our sins and escapes and loves and fears. And though we flee him for years, finally we may stop. And see.

That is awakening.

Awakening is when Jacob has an encounter with God and says, "Surely the LORD is in this place, and I wasn't aware of it" (Genesis 28:16).

Awakening happens for two disciples in the village of Emmaus when the resurrected Jesus appears to them. They don't recognize him at first; all they can see is dejection and defeat. He sits with them at an ordinary table and breaks bread and gives it to them, and then "their eyes were opened" (Luke 24:31). Luke uses the phrase from Genesis after the man and the woman disobey God, only this time eyes get opened to God and hope and life beyond death. "Were not our hearts burning within us?" they ask (verse 32).

For a friend of mine, awakening came in a bar, in a haze of alcohol, when his companion said there was zero chance of life after death. My friend suddenly realized he could no longer live in despair. He had hardly any real hope that God even existed, but he knew he could no longer sustain his life on a foundation of nothingness and death. He heard the first footsteps of the "hound of heaven." It was the beginning of the "acute fever" of faith.

In Alcoholics Anonymous, the twelfth and final step speaks of having had a "spiritual awakening":

When a man or a woman has a spiritual awakening, the most important meaning of it is that he has now become able to do, feel, and believe that which he could not do before on his unaided strength and resources alone. He has been granted a gift which amounts to a new state of consciousness and being. He has been set on a path which tells him he is really going somewhere, that life is not a dead end, not something to be endured or mastered. In a very real sense he has been transformed.[13]

Writer Bill Leonard notes that during what became known as the Second Great Awakening in the United States, conversion meant an awakened sense of identity and liberation in slave populations. A Kentucky slave woman named Winney was disciplined by the Forks of Elkhorn Baptist Church for "saying she once thought it her duty to serve her Master & Mistress but since the Lord had *converted her*, she had never believed that any Christian kept Negroes or slaves" and for adding "there was Thousands of white people Wallowing in Hell for their treatment to Negroes—she did not care if there was many more."[14] The church excommunicated the converted slave because she talked as one who was free!

Paul writes, "Wake up, sleeper, rise from the dead, and Christ will shine on you" (Ephesians 5:14). Christ's light serves both to awaken us from sleep and to illuminate our wakefulness.

With awakening comes the possibility not just of seeing the light but of becoming a part of it. Jesus himself told ordinary listeners, who by no means thought of themselves as spiritually radiant, "You are the light of the world. . . . Let your light shine before others, that they may see your good deeds and glorify your Father in heaven" (Matthew 5:14-16).

C. S. Lewis wrote how for many years the notion of "radiance" made no sense to him: "Who wishes to become a kind of living electric light bulb?" But he came to see what lies behind the image:

> We do not want merely to *see* beauty. . . . We want
> something else which can hardly be put into words—
> to be united with the beauty we see, to pass into it, to
> receive it into ourselves, to bathe in it, to become part
> of it. . . . Some day, God willing, we shall get *in*. When
> human souls have become as perfect in voluntary
> obedience as the inanimate creation is in its lifeless
> obedience, then they will put on its glory, or rather that
> greater glory of which Nature is only the first sketch.[15]

It is not by accident that we call celebrities "stars." Celebrity—to be known and affirmed by many—is a parody of our hunger to be known and affirmed by God. We long to hear, "Well done, good and faithful servant."

Jesus says, "Let your light shine." Jesus doesn't say, "Try harder to make your light shine." Lamps don't have to try hard. They just glow based on what's going on inside them. Paul writes that when we live according to God's light in our lives, the result is that "you will shine . . . like stars in the sky as you hold firmly to the word of life" (Philippians 2:15-16).

THE RESPONSE TO AWAKENING

Now that he's fully awake, Peter speaks.

The last time Matthew records Peter speaking is when he tells Jesus not to talk about the Cross. Jesus responded to him then: "Get behind me, Satan! You are a stumbling block to me; you do not have in mind the concerns of God, but merely human concerns" (Matthew 16:23).

So we might imagine that for six days Peter has been working on his mouth. For six days Peter has been telling himself, *I gotta be more careful next time. I'm not gonna shoot from the hip. Not gonna talk just to hear myself speak.* Yet here's what comes next: "Peter said to Jesus, 'Lord, it is good for us to be here. If you wish, I will put up three shelters—one for you, one for Moses and one for Elijah'" (Matthew 17:4).

Mark adds a little commentary: "He did not know what to say, they were so frightened" (Mark 9:6).

Apparently saying nothing did not occur to Peter.

You can see him trying to work on it:

- "Lord." (That's a good start.)
- "It's good for us to be here." (That's a little bland, but okay.)

- "If you wish . . ." ("Not my will"; that's good.)
- "I will make three booths; one for you, one for Moses, one for Elijah." (Huh?)

It's hard to know where to begin with this. One problem with this statement is that Peter misses the unique identity of Jesus and puts him on par with Moses and Elijah.

Another is a common problem with mountaintop experiences: Peter wants to stay on the mountain. It is possible to worship a spiritual or emotional *experience* of God rather than God himself.

Peter also tries to take control of the situation. But he was not invited up the mountain because he'd done something right, and he was not commanded off the mountain because he'd done something wrong. Peter doesn't realize that we are not in charge of the mountain; God is.

To make things worse, Peter's ego starts coming through. He doesn't say, "*We* will make booths"; he says, "*I* will make them." Too bad the other guys didn't think of it first.

And then there's just the folly of it. What are Jesus, Moses, and Elijah going to do with three booths? Sell bobblehead dolls?

Peter's blunders reveal an important truth: awakening does *not* mean we understand and think and say and do the right things. Actually, it's very much the contrary. Awakening usually starts with getting things wrong.

But God is patient with us: "While [Peter] was still speaking, a bright cloud covered them, and a voice from the cloud said, 'This is my Son, whom I love; with him I am well pleased. Listen to him!'" (Matthew 17:5).

There is a wonderful little detail here: "While [Peter] was still speaking." It's as if God is saying, "Hey, Peter, would you give it a rest for one minute?" Like if God waited for Peter to talk himself out, everyone would be gone.

I imagine Moses and Elijah asking Jesus, "Really—after four hundred years and a whole planet of people, this is the best you've got?"

God says now what he said when Jesus was baptized: "This is my Son, whom I love; with him I am well pleased."

When we awaken, ultimately, we awaken to love. The single fact the Father most wants the world to know is how lovable the Son is—all we have in the Son. In fact, the Voice adds one phrase here that wasn't said at Jesus' baptism, which Peter, James, and John are now ready to hear: *Listen to him.*

When? Every moment. Where? Every place. Why? He speaks truth with love. How? With a surrendered spirit. Do what he says.

Remember, awakening comes to us, if it comes at all, as a gift. You may have experienced it like this: You have a season when you long to worship God. Prayer comes easily to you, and God seems close enough to touch. Old temptations to lust or drink or gossip now look distasteful to you. You are motivated to read the Bible, you hunger to think noble thoughts. You feel energized for life. You want to be a better spouse or parent or friend. You are optimistic about the day. You find yourself grateful for simple gifts. Laughter comes easily.

This is awakening. Savor it. Enjoy it. Thank God for it. Learn from it. Build an altar of a little pile of stones so that you can remember it.

But don't insist on keeping it. Don't demand it. Don't worship it. Don't tie your obedience to it.

"*Listen to him.*" That is, do what Jesus says.

In other words, the response that God is looking for is not for us to relocate to the mountain permanently. It's not a continual vision of the Transfiguration. That vision comes, when it comes, for a moment, as a gift.

The right response to awakening is *obedience.* "Listen to him."

When we are given moments of closeness to God, our calling is not to try to prolong them. It's to surrender our wills.

The first three steps in Alcoholics Anonymous are a wonderful picture of this. In step 1, I awaken to my problem: my life is unmanageable, and I am powerless over my great enemy. In step 2, I awaken to my hope: I come to believe that God can restore me to moral sanity.

In step 3, I surrender: I turn my life and will over to God.

The proper response to the mountaintop isn't to try to stay on the mountaintop. It's to listen to the Son and do what he says.

When I try to picture this scene in my mind, it seems wonderful to me. I wish I could hear a voice from heaven that would remove all doubt and ground my faith forever. But whatever was going on, it did not produce joy and certainty in the hearts of the disciples: "When the disciples heard this, they fell facedown to the ground, terrified" (Matthew 17:6). They didn't want to see anymore. They didn't want to hear. They weren't glorified; they were petrified. And they were already disciples.

We awaken to fear as well as to glory. Isaiah saw the beauty and goodness of God—the lid was off the terrarium. But his cry was, "Woe to me! I am ruined! For I am a man of unclean lips, and I live among a people of unclean lips, and my eyes have seen the King, the LORD Almighty" (Isaiah 6:5).

This is why awakening is not just something that happens to us at the beginning of our spiritual lives. We need the gift of awakening each day. In Jesus' day, it was the people who considered themselves the most spiritually advanced whom he regarded as the most blind. Those who needed saving the most thought they needed it least. Thomas Merton wrote, "Truly the great problem is the salvation of those who, being good, think they have no further need to be saved and imagine their task is to make others 'good' like themselves!"[16]

Maybe God only gives me as much of him as I'm ready for.

After the disciples fell facedown, "Jesus came and touched them. 'Get up,' he said. 'Don't be afraid.' When they looked up, they saw no one except Jesus" (Matthew 17:7-8).

Jesus touches each one and tells them to get up. Falling on

your face is what you do when you die. Getting up is what you do when you get resurrected. The Kingdom has come near.

The Voice said they were to listen to Jesus. And the first thing Jesus says is not to condemn them, not to be harsh and severe. Rather, "Don't be afraid. It's me. It's still me. It's just me. Now you know."

Moses is gone. Elijah is gone. The cloud is gone. He's not glowing anymore. He's just regular old Jesus. The lesson is that the Law (Moses) and the Prophets (Elijah) all point to Jesus. Jesus is the one who "gets" them, who understands perfectly what their intent was.

Now they have to leave the mountaintop. They have to go back to their regular lives. There's work to do. In fact, the very next event in their lives is to go down from the mountain and meet a man whose son is suffering greatly and experience the disciples' failure to help him. They go from the mountaintop, not to another mountaintop, but to ordinary life, and work, and demands, and failure.

But here's the thing: Jesus is going with them.

And there will be other mountains.

In the middle of the desert, in Imperial County, California, by the Salton Sea, there is a mountain that doesn't belong there. It is an enormous piece of folk art called "Salvation Mountain." It is several stories high, made of adobe and straw and dirt and junk, topped with a cross, adorned with sayings like "Jesus is the way" and "God forgives sinners" and "God never fails."

It was constructed over decades by a man named Leonard Knight, who spent many years of his life doing odd jobs in the Midwest and for some reason decided the world needed Salvation Mountain. He labored year in and year out, through 115-degree days in the summer, and used over a hundred thousand gallons of paint. He was an ordinary, unschooled man.

His hope was to inspire people to know that God is love. No one seems to know what to make of it—whether it is art or kitsch or landfill. Yet people find themselves strangely drawn to make a pilgrimage there. Thousands of people come to Salvation Mountain from around the world and often leave some small item as a symbol of giving themselves to God.

Knight died a few years ago, but his mountain still stands.

Recently rock star Kesha recorded a song after experiencing hurt that was deep, personal, and public. It's called "Praying." It is raw and searing and honest. It begins with a voice-over that tries to make sense of the pain. "If there is a God or whatever . . . why have I been abandoned?" And then she sings, to the one who has hurt her, that she hopes he is praying as well.

Hurt and confusion, the ache for justice, the possibility of something beyond revenge.

She filmed the music video on Salvation Mountain.

There is another world.

It is not far away.

Things are not what they seem.

But awakening is only the beginning.

5

PURGATION
Leaving Baggage Behind

"Woe to me!" I cried. "I am ruined! For I am a man of
unclean lips, and I live among a people of unclean lips,
and my eyes have seen the King, the LORD Almighty."

ISAIAH 6:5

In *The Sickness unto Death*, Danish philosopher Søren Kierkegaard
describes the way sin blinds our self-awareness with a parable
about a peasant who once received enough money to buy shoes
and stockings and had enough left over to get drunk. On his way
home, he passed out in the road. A carriage came along, and the
driver told him to move or he would drive over his legs. The peasant woke, looked down at his legs, and did not recognize them
because of the shoes and stockings. "Go ahead," he said. "They
aren't my legs."[1]

Kierkegaard writes, "In the life of the spirit there is no
standing still; if a person does not do what is right the very

second he knows it is the right thing to do . . . the 'knowing' becomes more and more obscured."[2] I rationalize my behavior. I deny my intention. I "forget" the wrongs I've committed but memorize the wrongs I've received. How often in the news when people are caught in deceit or violence do they say, "That's not who I am"? But it *is* who I am. I have just convinced myself otherwise.

We do not recognize our own character. We do not see our own faults. We do not know our own souls.

"Go ahead. They aren't my legs."

As we have seen, our greatest need is not to be saved from what might happen *to* us but to be saved from what might happen *in* us; not from where we might end up but from who we might become.

Kierkegaard writes that sin is not simply breaking religious rules that we'd be better off without. It is not just doing wrong things but becoming the wrong person. Sin is "in despair not wanting to be oneself *before God*."[3] That's why he says the opposite of sin is not virtue. I may try to cultivate virtue on my own and still be in charge of my own life. The opposite of sin is faith: to be grounded transparently in God.[4]

God, in turn, doesn't hate sin because he's anti-pleasure. He invented pleasure. He hates sin because it promises so much and offers so little. Dr. Vincent Felitti wrote a remarkably profound explanation for the power of addiction: "It is hard to get enough of something that *almost* works."[5]

What we call addiction the Bible calls an idol. Alcohol almost works—until it doesn't. The same for success. Or money. Or comfort. Or any of the other glittering things we want to put on our bucket lists that still go by the old name of idols.

And so the journey to God leads through a process called purgation.

When a thought or feeling is buried deep within us, we will sometimes say we have to "get it out of our system." Sin has gotten into our system, and we cannot get it out on our own. Purgation is the process—never finished as long as we're on this side of the ground—by which God helps us get sin out of our system.

My friend Dallas Willard was eating once with a newly churched friend who popped a hot chili into his mouth and unwittingly said, "That'll burn the hell out of you." Dallas immediately replied, "Then give me a thousand of them."

Purgation is having the hell burned out of you.

It usually doesn't happen all at once but involves several components we'll look at in this chapter.

And this brings us to another story about Jesus and his followers. This one is about a lake, a boat, and a man. Something happened to that man, in that boat, in that lake. After he got out of that boat, he was not the same. The something that happened to him is something that always happens to people who come to intimacy with God. We never like the pain of it. But God knows we need it.

AWARENESS OF A HIGHER STANDARD

Here's how the story begins:

> One day as Jesus was standing by the Lake of
> Gennesaret, the people were crowding around him
> and listening to the word of God. He saw at the water's
> edge two boats, left there by the fishermen, who were
> washing their nets. He got into one of the boats, the
> one belonging to Simon, and asked him to put out
> a little from shore. Then he sat down and taught the
> people from the boat.
>
> LUKE 5:1-3

Jesus is teaching people about God and faith and the human condition. He loves people, so he's giving them wisdom about how to live. People are always hungry for this. Jesus is good at it, so pretty soon they are crowding in, and it looks like they are about to push him into the water.

Jesus sees two boats. He gets into one—apparently he knows Simon Peter and knows this is his boat—and says, "Simon, would you take me into the water so I can keep teaching?"

Peter rows him out a few feet.

Jesus sits down—maybe because it's hard to stand in a boat, maybe because to this day when rabbis are going to teach, they sit down so sermons can go on for a long, long, long time, which those of us who preach them often enjoy.

Try to imagine now what it was like to be Peter in that boat. I grew up in a Baptist church where they had giant chairs on the church platform, like thrones. Some of the church staff had to sit on those thrones through the whole sermon, and we used to watch to see who would fall asleep.

I wonder if Peter started to nod off—we know he got sleepy in the garden praying and on the Mount of Transfiguration, and we know he'd been up fishing all night long. He's probably fighting to keep his eyes open and wishing he'd brought some coffee.

Peter hears Jesus teaching the Word of God. We don't know what the content was.

Maybe "You are the light of the world." Peter thinks to himself, *I'd like for that to be true.*

Maybe it is about turning the other cheek. Peter, who will one day cut the ear off a man, thinks of all his anger issues.

Maybe it is "Let your yes be yes and your no be no." Peter, who will one day lie about even knowing Jesus, thinks of all the lies he's told.

Maybe it is "Don't worry about your life." Peter, who will one day panic on this very lake with Jesus, thinks of all his faithless fears.

Maybe for Peter, as he hears Jesus talk, there's this strange combination of hope about what he might be and shame about how far he's fallen short. Every human being has to decide what *standard* they will aspire to. The biblical writers generally, and

Jesus in unmatched fashion, describe the divine standard for human fulfillment. People may be inspired by this, or intimidated, or angered, or depressed, or offended. But to hear it includes the awareness that we don't measure up.

Jesus finishes, and Peter begins rowing Jesus back to shore, maybe commenting on how well the talk went.

But Jesus has other plans. "When he had finished speaking, he said to Simon, 'Put out into deep water, and let down the nets for a catch'" (Luke 5:4).

Have you ever had a situation where you're an expert on something—it's your job—and people who are amateurs start giving you advice?

Peter's a professional fisherman. Jesus is a carpenter-turned-rabbi. Peter could have said, "Hey, Jesus—I won't tell you how to give talks, and you don't tell me how to catch fish." He could have told Jesus, "It's the wrong place; I've just been working it" or "It's the wrong time; fish don't bite in broad daylight" or "It's the wrong crew; my guys are exhausted."

Instead, Peter says, "Master, we've worked hard all night and haven't caught anything. But because you say so, I will let down the nets" (Luke 5:5).

He calls Jesus "Master." It's Peter's boat, but he puts it at Jesus' disposal. He is aware that he is in the presence of a person and power greater than himself. He does what Jesus wants him to do rather than what he would normally do himself.

This is an act of faith. "Because you say so . . ." Peter doesn't see what Jesus sees, but he's willing to do what Jesus says. And that's enough for Jesus: "When they had done so, they caught such a large number of fish that their nets began to break. So they signaled their partners in the other boat to come and help them, and they came and filled both boats so full that they began to sink" (Luke 5:6-7).

Boats nowadays have fish finders, which send out up to two hundred thousand sound waves per second and let you locate fish with amazing accuracy. Apparently Jesus had one of these built in. Jesus could have been the greatest fisherman of all time. He could have been the greatest *anything* of all time. He knew where the fish were, or he just willed them into the boat. Either way, it must have been fun. As I read this story, I was thinking how much Jesus must have enjoyed being Jesus. We're drawn to people who love their lives and their work. I imagine at a moment like this, Jesus was just sitting there with a big smile on his face. "Told ya so."

This must have been an amazing moment. We wonder how a fisherman might respond in such circumstances. "Beginner's luck." Or "Wow. Thanks." Or "Same time tomorrow?" I expect if I had been Peter, it would have occurred to me that if I could partner with Jesus every day, I would soon be rich. But getting rich is trivial to Jesus. He has bigger fish to fry.

Peter responds in none of these ways. "When Simon Peter saw this . . ."

By the way, this is the only time Luke uses his full name.

When I was a kid, if I got called by my full name—"John Carl Ortberg Jr., get in here!"—guess what it meant? Trouble. Full-name treatment meant then what it means now: "I know exactly who you are, and don't think you can hide."

"When Simon Peter saw this, he fell at Jesus' knees and said, 'Go away from me, Lord; I am a sinful man'" (Luke 5:8).

CONFESSION

This is a dramatic moment. Peter doesn't even take the time to kneel; he falls at Jesus' knees the way a condemned peasant might with a king. The floor of the boat is covered with fish, and he doesn't even notice.

He asks Jesus to leave him. He says he is a sinful man.

In our day we're apt to look at this and say, "Hey, where's your sense of self-esteem? Don't let religion make you feel bad about yourself."

Part of our problem in understanding how the journey of purgation works lies here: we may say the words that Peter says, but we are not apt to feel what Peter feels.

To capture Peter's feelings, it would be helpful to go to an Alcoholics Anonymous meeting and watch someone who has been a drunk for thirty years; who has lost career and marriage and self-respect; who has been in jails and treatment programs and bankruptcy court; who has thrown up on the furniture and urinated in the clothes hamper in the middle of the night;

who has fought against saying these words with every scrap of strength for decades while watching his life be destroyed, sit in a room full of other drunks and for the first time say the words that will crush him and then bring him life: "My name is Peter. I'm an alcoholic."

Those words are death; they are the end of one life. But they are life—the beginning of another. They have been avoided every day until now. From this day forward, they will be remembered and cherished. Around the circle, the other members of AA will say, "Hi, Peter."

They are celebrating with him—not that he has a drinking problem but that he has recognized and acknowledged that he has a problem he can't control. They realize, as Kent Dunnington has noted, that the recognition and public acknowledgment of inadequacy is itself an irreplaceable spiritual achievement.[6]

Some churches have a public confession of sin. When this is working right, the confession of sin is to a church what "My name is John, and I'm an alcoholic" is to AA. But it seldom works right these days. *Sinner* no longer packs the punch it once did. We don't dread saying it. We can say it without wincing. Acknowledging sin no longer means we have to change something in the way that acknowledging alcoholism does. A drinker who says those words understands that, because God is gracious, everything in their life is about to change. A church person who says, "I'm a sinner" generally *mis*understands it to mean that because God is gracious, nothing in their life has to change at all.

Often today we think of grace as a mere release from consequences. But grace is about something much bigger than not getting punished. If we think of salvation primarily in legal terms of being proclaimed innocent, it leaves our inner persons untouched and unchanged. It makes us think we can want grace without wanting Jesus.

In fact, genuine repentance never takes as its primary aim the avoidance of punishment. Another story about a man and a boat and a confession comes from the wonderfully colorful sermon on Jonah in *Moby-Dick*: "And here, shipmates, is true and faithful repentance; not clamorous for pardon, but grateful for punishment."[7]

David Brooks suggests that our society has been shifting from a culture of humility to what might be called a culture of the Big Me. For instance, in 1950 when Gallup asked high school seniors if they considered themselves very important, 12 percent said yes. Fifty-five years later, 80 percent considered themselves very important. Today 93 percent of young people score higher on a narcissism test than the middle score of just twenty years ago. In the bestselling *Eat, Pray, Love* (which Brooks is the only man to admit he has finished), Elizabeth Gilbert writes that God is manifested through "my own voice from within myself. . . . God dwells within you as you yourself, exactly the way you are."[8]

But perhaps we're whistling in the dark. Maybe we know better. It's hard to get enough of what almost works.

Christian writers across the centuries have said that pride—typified by the Big Me—is at the core of our spiritual problem. C. S. Lewis writes, "Unchastity, anger, greed, drunkenness, and all that, are mere flea bites in comparison: it was through Pride that the devil became the devil: Pride leads to every other vice. It is the complete anti-God state of mind. . . . That raises a terrible question. How is it that people who are quite obviously eaten up with Pride can say they believe in God and appear to themselves very religious? I am afraid it means they are worshipping an imaginary God."[9]

Neal Plantinga notes a great change regarding pride in our day, which makes pursuing purgation harder. Not that pride is going away—"People still have affairs with themselves. Professors still leave faculty meetings feeling less enlightened by what they heard than by what they said." Rather, "What has changed is that, in much of contemporary American culture, aggressive self-regard is no longer viewed with alarm." He notes that Jesus did not say, "Woe to you, poor scribes and Pharisees! Nice guys but your self-esteem is low." Nor did Paul write, "Neither circumcision counts for anything nor uncircumcision, but feeling good about yourselves."[10]

Peter says, "Go away from me, Lord; I am a sinful man" (Luke 5:8). He has a profound experience of Jesus' identity, and this causes a profound awareness of his own brokenness.

We humans have a profound, mysterious, unfixable tendency to foul things up. And when I encounter Jesus, I realize that the problem isn't just other people; *I* have a profound, mysterious, unfixable tendency to foul things up too.

The response is confession. In confession, we seek not simply a vague acknowledgment of general guilt but concrete examples of our real-time character defects.

I believe in each of us is a closet called "shame." In that closet we hide the memories or weaknesses that mortify us. Sex, maybe. Or alcohol. Or big lies. Or stealing. Or simply shame at being who we are. The strangest thing happens when what we have most wanted to conceal is brought into the open. We don't die. Instead, we often begin to heal.

A pastor friend was caught plagiarizing his messages. He was disciplined and had to apologize publicly. Everybody knows about it now. And a few days afterward, I noticed the strangest thing: instead of being depressed, there was a lightness in him I had never seen before. Then I understood. It was the years of hiding and faking and deceiving that were weighing him down. Now that there was nothing to hide, now that everybody knew the worst about him, shame turned to relief. It's actually lighter to be known for who you really are than to be admired for who you're really not.

When a driver behind me got mad about how long my parallel parking job caused him to be stuck in traffic, he pulled up next to me, rolled down his window, and asked, "What's your problem?" The encounter only lasted a few seconds, but his question has stuck with me for years.

Charles Taylor notes that any belief system that affirms human life when it goes right has to account for what happens when it goes wrong. "What's your problem?" For many centuries in the part of the world influenced by Jesus, people would answer that question with the word *sin*. In our day we tend to use the language of *sickness*. Moral language has shifted to therapeutic language. Words like *cheater* or *liar* or *adulterer* sound Victorian and melodramatic, but we don't mind admitting to "issues" of fear or anxiety or addiction.

One irony in this is that the therapeutic culture from Freud on wanted to free people from the "illusion" of religion, but "now we are forced to go to new experts, therapists, doctors who exercise the kind of control that is appropriate over blind and compulsive mechanisms."[11] As James K. A. Smith writes, "In the name of securing our freedom, we swap submission to the priest for submission to the therapist."[12]

A deeper irony is that when we shift from the moral domain to the therapeutic, we actually *lose* freedom. We move from responsibility to victimhood. A colleague of mine kept running into a personal problem she could not solve. Her comment was "I'm more of a headcase than I thought." Both of us have been immersing ourselves in the Twelve Steps, which place a major emphasis on responsibility. Paradoxically, we have both found that examining our problems as accountable moral agents who need God actually *decreases* our sense of victimhood and *increases* strength. Sickness and the need for healing are a deep part of our problem but not the deepest part. What is unique about sin is that it does not just happen *to* us; it happens *in* us. The deepest part of the person is the will, and the will can choose sin until it gets embedded in our bodies. Sin carries a moral weight that illness—no matter how awful—does not.

REMORSE

Peter is not simply aware of his sin. His actions—to fall to his knees, to verbalize his condition, to feel pain in Jesus' presence—are expressions of remorse. The word *remorse*, like the word *sin*, has fallen on hard times. It is often taken as a sign of health to say, "I have no regrets." But any sane human being is full of them.

For judges and prosecutors, it matters greatly if a wrongdoer shows signs of remorse or seems to be truly sorry. (It matters for parents and spouses, too!) Why is that? It is because "the person who can harm others and feel no remorse is, indeed, a different kind of person from the one who is sorry."[13] So James says, "Wash your hands, you sinners, and purify your hearts, you double-minded. Grieve, mourn and wail" (James 4:8-9). This is not an invitation to morbidity. It is an invitation to humanity.

Of course, it does no good to try to conjure up miserable feelings. What I can do is look at my harmful words and deeds from the perspective of those I've hurt and from the perspective of the God who loves them (and me). Healthy remorse is a by-product of the empathic reflection of recovering sinners.

Purgation is always about freedom. With addiction, purgation involves freedom from the compulsion to use or drink or gamble or buy or look. I tend to think cutting myself off from my secret sins will leave me in misery, but when I begin to discover the reality of Jesus and his Kingdom and the health of being known, appetites that were once my master can now take their rightful place as servants. I am free from my compulsions and free to think and want more interesting things.

And the purpose of this is healing.

I went to my dermatologist recently. He looked at my skin with a trained eye, a magnifying glass, and special lights. He told me, "You have years of sun damage—back to when you were a kid. It's gotten under your skin. You can't see it—I can. Untreated, it'll kill you."

I'm carrying sun death under my skin. Day after day, year after year, exposed to the sun with no sunblock, no hat, no zinc oxide. Whose fault is that? My mom and dad's fault, obviously. They should have shaded me. It's my Scandinavian genes. It's the ozone layer. It's all of these. But it's me, too. How many times did I decide not to do what I knew I should do?

Then my dermatologist said, "Next time you come, we'll put chemicals like acid on your face, then sit you under a special heat lamp. It'll hurt till you can't take it anymore—then it will hurt worse."

In purgation, that's called repentance. It's not pain for pain's sake. It's healing that may temporarily hurt. I allow blemishes to come to the surface so they may be healed by the light.

Paul said that Jesus' plan is to free us from this sin power until we are "without stain or wrinkle or any other blemish" (Ephesians 5:27). Truthfully, I'd be fine with some blemishes. But not my doctor. Why not? It isn't because he has unreasonable standards. It's because those blemishes will kill me.

Paul writes, "Do not let any unwholesome talk come out of your mouths. . . . Get rid of all bitterness, rage and anger, brawling and slander, along with every form of malice" (Ephesians 4:29-31). Which of those would I like to hang on to? I sometimes deceive myself into thinking I can't live without these things, but under Christ's light, I recognize them for what they are: death.

MAKING AMENDS

Making amends—seeking to set right what you have done wrong—is a central practice for spiritual health. It was commanded in the book of Leviticus. If anyone defrauded someone by deceit or robbery or even finding someone's wallet and lying about it, "They must make restitution in full, and add a fifth of the value to it, and give it all to the owner on the day they present their guilt offering" (Leviticus 6:5).

Sadly, some people following the minimum-entrance-requirements gospel believe that grace means never having to make amends. But that is not what happens when people meet Jesus.

When Jesus came into the life of a tax collector named Zacchaeus, Zacchaeus, like Peter, realized the extent to which he did not live up to the standard of his true identity. His response was a joyful amends: he publicly vowed he would pay back anyone not what he owed plus 20 percent, but *four times what he owed*, and in addition he would give half his possessions to the poor (see Luke 19:8). One imagines Mrs. Zacchaeus saying, "Shouldn't we maybe have talked about this ahead of time?"

Making amends is not a violation of grace; it is a means of grace. It is what love would do. It seeks to right those I have wronged and am now called to love. And it helps me to change. This is why the eighth and ninth steps in Alcoholics Anonymous are to first become willing to make amends and then (as possible) to actually make them.

If I owe someone money, I pay them back. If I have gossiped about someone, I confess it and ask their forgiveness. If I have lied to someone, I acknowledge my lie and tell them the truth. I had to return to a coworker recently and tell them I'd lied about not having accidentally left confidential material on their desk when that was exactly what I'd done. One of the wonderful gifts of making amends is it helps to free us from the ridiculous idea that our characters are above questioning. Our characters need to be questioned!

FORMING A NEW INTENTION

Peter is suddenly, unsuspectingly caught. He's in the hands of the law. He's been found out. It's so interesting: his request of Jesus is "Go away. Please leave. Don't look at me again, or talk to me again, or think of me again." He asks to be forever excluded from Jesus' presence.

What if Jesus had said yes to that request?

But Jesus always sees beyond our words to our hearts. Jesus always sees beyond what we ask to what we really need.

Jesus says to Peter, "Don't be afraid. The very confession of sin that you think disqualifies you is just what I was waiting for to be able to use you. You are forgiven. You can be whole. I want you free."

Jesus doesn't deny Peter's sinfulness, but he gives him a new vocation, a new *intention*—to become the kind of person who can spread the Kingdom, who can catch people instead of fish.

The new intention we receive as part of gaining freedom from sin is the intention to follow Jesus. Most simply, it's that we put obeying Jesus above all else.

Jesus often spoke of the need for this intention:

Not everyone who says to me "Lord, Lord," will enter the kingdom of heaven, but only the one who does the will of my Father.

MATTHEW 7:21

Why do you call me "Lord, Lord," and not do what
I say?

LUKE 6:46

Anyone who chooses to do the will of God will find
out whether my teaching comes from God.

JOHN 7:17

If you love me, keep my commands.

JOHN 14:15

If you keep my commands, you will remain in my love.

JOHN 15:10

Jesus never pauses to reassure people (as so many preachers
do) that, of course, it's okay to not even intend to obey him as
long as you believe the right things. This is why Dallas Willard
used to call the phrase "teaching them to *obey* everything I have
commanded you" the great *omission* from what is often called
the great commission (see Matthew 28:18-20).

Obedience has become the virtue that nobody wants. How
many teachers write a note to parents congratulating them
on having an extraordinarily obedient child? How many parents would be happy to receive such a note? We want leaders,
mavericks, rogue agents, and nonconformists who don't care
about other people's opinions (although we want this for our

children so other people will think well of them—and of us as their parents). When is the last time you saw a bumper sticker that said, "My Child Is an Obedient Student at High Achievers Elementary School"?

To us, obedience smacks of compliance. It doesn't sound like a leadership trait. Often we associate obedience with unthinking, robotic conformity to rules that might make us less human.

But that's compliance, not obedience as Jesus called for it. The obedience Jesus called for requires judgment, discernment, creativity, and initiative. It's about becoming an excellent *person*, not an excellent *rule follower*. In fact, an obsessive concern with following rules will hinder your development into becoming the kind of person who does what Jesus says. Dallas Willard once said, "A person can become so obsessed with doing what Jesus said that they fail to become the kind of person Jesus wants."[14]

A simple old song is hard to improve on:

Trust and obey, for there's no other way
To be happy in Jesus, but to trust and obey.

We have too often turned it into another way: "Trust—and you don't have to obey!" But trust that doesn't obey isn't trust at all. It's a mental game to say otherwise. It is the nature of genuine trust to obey; that's what trust *means*.

There *is* no other way. And it's not true about just Jesus. There's no other way to be happy in your doctor, or your trainer, or your vocal coach, or your auto mechanic. If you trust that they are competent, you are prepared to do what they say. What else would it mean to trust them?

A disciple is someone who, above all, seeks to obey Jesus—intelligently, responsibly, and creatively, with initiative and enthusiasm and flair.

I always want to have my own way. That's why it's called *my* way. But the Bible calls living to have our own way "the way of the wicked." It does not lead to the Good Place.

Obedience is the way of purgation. It is the way to be happy in Jesus.

There is no other.

DAILY SHALOM CHECK

For Peter, this time with Jesus in the boat is the first confession of his sin, but it will not be his last. He will tempt Jesus with the words of Satan; he will fail to trust Jesus on the water; he will cut off somebody's ear; when Jesus needs him most, he will deny him three times. Even after Jesus is gone and the Holy Spirit has come, Peter will need to be cured of his ethnocentrism before he can truly accept a Gentile named Cornelius, and Paul will have to confront him about catering to some legalists. Being honest about and seeking healing for my sin will be part of me the rest of my life.

Earlier I talked about the necessary treatment I have to

undergo at my dermatologist for sun damage. Do I have to go through that light torture only one time? Nope. How often do I have to go through the treatment? Until the blemishes are healed.

Paul wrote, "Not that I have already obtained all this, or have already been made perfect" (Philippians 3:12)—and he was an apostle. Discipleship is a whole-life endeavor. Hurry does not help. "All God's processes are slow. The works of God take time and cannot be rushed."[15]

I regularly make sure my skin is getting examined—new problems keep popping up. Similarly, I make sure I'm regularly going through healing—that means confession; that means being willing for God to correct my shortcomings; that means making amends to people I've hurt. It's ongoing.

And this is part of salvation. Dallas Willard writes,

The consumer Christian is one who utilizes the grace of God for forgiveness and the services of the church for special occasions, but does not give his or her life and innermost thoughts, feelings, and intentions over to the kingdom of the heavens. Such Christians are not inwardly transformed and not committed to it. Because this is so, they remain not just "imperfect," for all of us remain imperfect, but routinely and seriously unable and unwilling to do the good they know to do. . . . They remain *governed*, or "slaves" of . . . sin.[16]

Neal Plantinga writes that being freed from sin from day to day involves what might be called "spiritual hygiene": "Although it sounds as if it might have something to do with the brushing and flossing away of small particles of vice, spiritual hygiene is actually wholeness of spirit—that is, wholeness of what animates and characterizes us."[17] That wholeness is *shalom*.[18]

So I engage in practices through which I'm given the power to respond to life in new ways. One way to think of these practices—spiritual disciplines—is that they are things I do with my body that suspend my habitual patterns of thinking and feeling and so make space for God.

Do I constantly hurry and rush? Then I deliberately get in the longest line at the grocery store and remind myself that "all God's processes are slow."

Do I constantly crave approval? Then I go by myself to the ocean and remind myself that the waves were coming in long before I was born and will come in long after I die, and God and his Kingdom are doing very well. I can feel some of his approval seeping into my synapses.

Do I constantly grumble? I take time to be aware of what produces honest gratitude. I celebrate it. I write it down. I tell others about it.

Do I lie, lust, or self-promote? I stop hiding. I acknowledge it to God, fearlessly and searchingly. I ask him to help me see more as I am able.

Plantinga writes, "A spiritually sound person disciplines her life by such spiritual exercises as prayer, fasting, confession, worship, and reflective walks through cemeteries. She visits boring persons and tries to take an interest in them, ponders the lives of saints and compares them to her own, spends time and money on just and charitable causes."[19] Engaging in these disciplines helps us each day to purge those parts of our lives that are not in alignment with Jesus and to walk closer in step with him.

THE UNIVERSAL LEAGUE OF THE GUILTY

God, we are told, is light. Light reveals what is hidden. When we encounter the light of God, even in small ways, our twistedness and duplicity and tendency to foul up are revealed. Our denial and collusion stand naked before us.

Peter says, "Get away from me, Lord. I am a sinful man."

Jesus smiles again. This is his favorite part of the job.

He doesn't say, "Peter, I had no idea. Let me off this boat at once!"

We get so weird with God. People lie or steal or go to adult websites but never want to talk about it with God. Do you think God doesn't already know? Do you think God is shocked when you confess? "I had no idea. *You*—off the boat!"

Instead, Jesus says, "Don't be afraid; from now on you will fish for people" (Luke 5:10).

It is as though Jesus didn't hear Peter. It is as though Jesus thinks that what Peter just said somehow qualifies him to go out and help people. Because to Jesus, it did.

"I am a sinful man." It is this genuine, transparent confession that enables us to be used by God and used with surprising power. As long as it is in Peter's heart, it will keep him from despising others, as religious people—including Christians!—so often do. Peter's statement is a reminder that there is not one group of people who are good and another group of people who are evil. Rather, before Jesus, all of us are sinners.

The recognition and public confession of inadequacy is a spiritual achievement; more than that, it's a great gift to others.

And this is how intimacy deepens. Remember—intimacy is shared experience. The experience of our shame and guilt is what we *least* want to share. It comes to others as a gift of great cost, because they could hurt us with it. And in the strange alchemy of Jesus' Kingdom, intimacy gets built around the confession and forgiveness of sin like nothing else. There is more intimacy in one deep confession than a thousand résumés of achievement.

Jesus is going to be Peter's friend and teacher in spite of Peter's sinful condition. This is salvation. But salvation is more than simply a declaration of legal status.

We are, in the words of one writer, part of the Universal League of the Guilty.

We don't pretend perfection.

We don't get discouraged by setbacks and relapses.

But we are on the road.

Every once in a while, as with Peter, when we're in the boat, Jesus shows up; we are undone again by who he is; and we get a deeper look at the trouble under our skin. And he gives us a fresh treatment under the light that stings for a moment but heals for life.

In both this story and the story of the Transfiguration, the disciples see spiritual reality in a new way and are terrified. Both times Jesus tells them, "Don't be afraid." It is his most common command because our fears will keep us from God. Our fears are behind many of our sins. John says that "perfect love casts out fear" (1 John 4:18, NRSV). And when love begins to outweigh fear, we move into a new stage of our journey toward God. We are illumined by love.

6

ILLUMINATION
A New Mental Map

To hold to a doctrine or an opinion with the intellect alone
is not to believe it. A man's real belief is that which he lives by.

GEORGE MACDONALD

Illumination comes to us, if it comes at all, as a gift. I don't
know of a better picture of it than from the autobiography of
Helen Keller. She writes that the day her teacher came to her
was the most important day of her life. "I am filled with wonder
when I consider the immeasurable contrasts between the two
lives which it connects."[1]

Illumination is the word for the process by which we come
to see and think differently. A new world becomes available that
was previously closed to us. Often this happens gradually; for
Helen Keller it came in a single day:

One day, while I was playing with my new doll, Miss
Sullivan put my big rag doll into my lap also, spelled

"d-o-l-l" and tried to make me understand that "d-o-l-l" applied to both. Earlier in the day we had had a tussle over the words "m-u-g" and "w-a-t-e-r." Miss Sullivan had tried to impress it upon me that "m-u-g" is *mug* and that "w-a-t-e-r" is *water*, but I persisted in confounding the two.

In despair she had dropped the subject for the time, only to renew it at the first opportunity. I became impatient at her repeated attempts and, seizing the new doll, I dashed it upon the floor. I was keenly delighted when I felt the fragments of the broken doll at my feet. Neither sorrow nor regret followed my passionate outburst. I had not loved the doll. In the still, dark world in which I lived there was no strong sentiment or tenderness.

I felt my teacher sweep the fragments to one side of the hearth, and I had a sense of satisfaction that the cause of my discomfort was removed. She brought me my hat, and I knew I was going out into the warm sunshine. This thought, if a wordless sensation may be called a thought, made me hop and skip with pleasure.

We walked down the path to the well-house, attracted by the fragrance of the honeysuckle with which it was covered. Some one was drawing water and my teacher placed my hand under the spout. As the cool stream gushed over one hand she spelled into the other the word *water*, first slowly, then rapidly.

I stood still, my whole attention fixed upon the motions of her fingers. Suddenly I felt a misty consciousness as of something forgotten—a thrill of returning thought; and somehow the mystery of language was revealed to me.

I knew then that "w-a-t-e-r" meant the wonderful cool something that was flowing over my hand. That living word awakened my soul, gave it light, hope, joy, set it free! There were barriers still, it is true, but barriers that could in time be swept away.

I left the well-house eager to learn. Everything had a name, and each name gave birth to a new thought. As we returned to the house every object which I touched seemed to quiver with life. That was because I saw everything with the strange, new sight that had come to me.

On entering the door I remembered the doll I had broken. I felt my way to the hearth and picked up the pieces. I tried vainly to put them together. Then my eyes filled with tears; for I realized what I had done, and for the first time I felt repentance and sorrow.

I learned a great many new words that day. I do not remember what they all were; but I do know that *mother*, *father*, *sister*, *teacher* were among them—words that were to make the world blossom for me, "like Aaron's rod, with flowers."

It would have been difficult to find a happier child than I was as I lay in my crib at the close of that eventful day and lived over the joys it had brought me, and for the first time longed for a new day to come.[2]

Helen had been alone, and now she was not. She had been imprisoned in her mind, and now she was set free. She had been trapped in anger and self-pity, and now she knew repentance. She had felt useless, and now she had a great purpose that would inspire millions. Her world blossomed, and she along with it.

And it happened because of one person. After the water had been sprinkled on her, she made Miss Sullivan her friend and teacher and guide. She did what Miss Sullivan said. She learned what Miss Sullivan taught. She was saved.

"That living word awakened my soul, gave it light, hope, joy, set it free!"

This is illumination.

POP QUIZ

We are in school with Jesus' disciples. A disciple is simply a learner. Jesus is our teacher. He is not just a teacher, but his teaching is central to his life. His teaching is one of the ways through which he is our Savior, through which he saves us from a life of blindness and despair and impatience and brokenness and isolation.

One day Jesus took his students to where the water flowed. It was a place called Caesarea Philippi, famous for the water that flowed from Mount Hermon down to Jericho. Jesus—who, whatever else you think about him, was clearly a remarkable teacher—decided to give his students a pop quiz.

In another book, I told my favorite pop quiz story from a class on ornithology. Students were told they had to identify twenty-five species of birds, but all they had to go on was pictures of the birds' feet. One student snapped under the pressure and refused to take the test. When the teacher told the student he'd flunk and asked him his name, he rolled his pants to his knees and said, "You tell me!"

The value of pop quizzes is that they reveal what we really know and not just what we cram for and soon forget. They come without warning. Your significant other asks, "Where do you see this relationship headed?" In the elevator your company's intense CEO asks, "What are you working on today?"

Jesus' most famous pop quiz features this central question: "Who do you say that I am?" It's amazing that two thousand years after his life, people are still wrestling with that question.

How would you answer? How would you answer in your heart of hearts if it weren't on the test and no one knew what you'd say, if there were no pressure to give the "right answer"?

There is a widespread belief that Christians are people who

give what they think is the right answer to that question, and non-Christians are people who give what Christians think is the wrong answer to that question.

But as it turns out, Jesus himself didn't approach the question that way. What you think about Jesus matters immensely, but not for the reasons many people think. God's main goal for you—and the way you become intimate with God—is not actually that you can give the right answer. It's something deeper. So let's get into the story.

The setting for this pop quiz is crucial. Caesarea Philippi was on the northernmost border of Israel. It was under the authority of Herod Philip. Most of Jesus' ministry took place in Galilee, which was under the authority of Herod Agrippa. Herod Agrippa seduced the wife of his brother and married her. Herod Agrippa was also the man who killed John the Baptist and wanted to kill Jesus. Both Philip and Agrippa were sons of Herod the Great. The stolen wife of Herod Agrippa was actually a granddaughter of Herod the Great, whose name was Herodias. (Herod the Great apparently named everybody after himself.)

John the Baptist said to Herod Agrippa, "You shouldn't seduce your brother's wife, especially when she's also your niece." That's part of why Herod Agrippa had John's head sliced off and why he was now after Jesus. (It was more or less an ancient reality show: *The Real Housewives of Herod*.)

Automatically, anyone Herod Agrippa *didn't* like, Herod

Philip liked. So this region was a safe place for Jesus. He wasn't being hunted here. It was a good place to have a reflective conversation.

But there's more going on.

The reason there was a city here at all is water. To this day there is a huge cave with a refreshing stream flowing nearby. We're told by the historian Josephus that in ancient times so much water gushed out, they couldn't measure the depth of the pool. In the ancient world, where water was sacred, this became a center for religious shrines.

Centuries before Jesus was born, this became a place where the god Baal was worshiped. There are remains of at least fourteen temples to him in the area. Baal was a fertility god whose worship included both cultic prostitution and human sacrifice.

After Baal, Caesarea Philippi became associated with the Greek god Pan—its old name was "Panion." The Greeks said Pan was born in the cave here. Pan was half man, half goat, and his mother was so revolted by this that she abandoned him. So Pan was associated with chaos and disorder. He would throw your enemies into *pan*ic. He would create *pan*demonium (a spirit or demon of chaos). He would later inspire *pan*cakes— cakes with all the height and goodness flattened out of them.

You can still see niches around the cave where there were statues to the pagan gods Hermes and Echo. There's a sign that describes how human sacrifices were sent to the realm of the dead (to the Greeks it was known as Hades). There's a line of thought that since this cave was believed to be the entrance to the underworld, it was known as the "gates of Hades."

Caesar Augustus had given this city to Herod the Great. Herod built a giant temple for emperor worship there. When Herod Philip inherited the city, he renamed it "Caesarea Philippi"—"Caesarea" to honor Caesar, "Philippi" to honor himself.

What's more, the spring at Caesarea Philippi was believed to be the primary source of the River Jordan, the most important river in Israel—the river God parted for Joshua and where John baptized Jesus.

The human race has always wanted to know, What's our story? Who is our God? Why are we here? Where are we headed?

Jesus and the disciples come here. Maybe they're looking at that cave. It's like Jesus is saying, "I want you to consider all the claims of all the powers and religions people have explored."

Jesus starts his pop quiz with a safe question. "When Jesus came to the region of Caesarea Philippi, he asked his disciples, 'Who do people say the Son of Man is?'" (Matthew 16:13).

The disciples answer, "Some say John the Baptist; others say Elijah; and still others, Jeremiah or one of the prophets" (Matthew 16:14). People were hoping God would send one of their heroes back to them.

"But what about you?" Jesus asks them. "Who do you say I am?" (Matthew 16:15).

This is like the final question on *Jeopardy*. The pressure is on. They're all looking at their feet. Everybody had an answer to the first question. Not so much this time.

Let's pause here, because there's a lot going on.

I believe Jesus asks them who they think he is because he wants to know who they think he is. (I know—deep.) In other words, they haven't told him. They've been fuzzy. They've had countless conversations with him about God, life, love, the Kingdom. But this is the first time he asks them directly what they believe about his identity.

At the beginning of their relationship, Jesus didn't say, "Believe the right things about me, and you can be my disciples."

He said, "Follow me, and you'll be my disciples" (see Matthew 4:18-19).

In other words, "If you choose to follow me, you'll come to know me. If you do not choose to follow me, it doesn't really matter what you say you believe about me."

What matters most to Jesus is not that I'm a believer about him; it's that I'm a follower of him.

THE FAITH OF JESUS CHRIST

Many people have the notion that life with Jesus starts by affirming certain beliefs about him—beliefs about his divinity and about his death. Christianity is thought to be a "bounded set," where belief separates insiders from outsiders.

Jesus himself didn't teach that. He didn't go to people initially and say, "Believe the right stuff about me, and eventually you might want to follow me." He said, "Follow me, and eventually you'll come to believe the right stuff." He called people to make following him the *center* of their lives.

Here's where this is good news for you. You might be thinking, *Honestly, I'm not sure what I believe about Jesus. I'm not sure I believe a human being could be divine. I'm afraid that means I'm out.*

Not at all. People sometimes think *faith* means trying to will yourself to believe what you know isn't true. In *Through the Looking-Glass*, Alice tells the White Queen, "One can't believe impossible things." The Queen replies, "I daresay you haven't had much practice. When I was your age, I always did it for half-an-hour a day. Why, sometimes I've believed as many as six impossible things before breakfast."[3] Belief is simply not the sort of thing you can *make* yourself do. And Jesus would be the first to say you must follow the truth wherever it leads.

Illumination doesn't simply mean believing certain things *about* Jesus. It means coming to believe *what Jesus himself believed.*

In another pop quiz, Jesus got into a boat with the disciples. A furious storm arose, but Jesus slept through it. His disciples woke him: "Teacher, don't you care if we drown?"

He rebuked the wind, and the waves were still. He then called his disciples "Little-faiths," a nickname he made up to gently chide them. "Why are you so afraid?" he asked them (see Matthew 8:23-26).

Note that in the storm, the disciples went to Jesus. They believed he might be able to do something, but they didn't have enough faith to take a nap. They did not believe what Jesus believed—that they were safe the whole time.

Richard Hays wrote one of the most influential books on the New Testament in the last forty years, *The Faith of Jesus Christ*, in which he argues that the phrase often translated "faith *in* Jesus Christ" is best translated "the faith *of* Jesus Christ"—that is, the faithfulness and belief system of Jesus.[4]

It turns out that it's tricky to know what I truly believe.

Here's one way to see this. Years ago my friend Danny invited me to go paragliding off a cliff for my birthday. I had heard about how safe the wing was and how the lines were secure and the hooks were strong. When I was sitting back far away from the edge of the cliff, I thought I believed what I'd heard.

When I got to the edge, what do you think happened to my belief that paragliding was safe? My knees didn't believe it. My palms and armpits didn't believe it. I pictured myself squashed flat, dead, on the ground. I pictured my children without a father, my wife dating other men—younger and handsomer men. It turns out that as the edge got closer, my belief got weaker.

We might put beliefs into two categories:

1. There are things we *think* we believe until we get to the edge of the cliff and that belief is tested.
2. Then there is our mental map about how things are. This is what we actually believe.

You never violate your mental map about the way things are. You live at the mercy of your mental map.

For instance, I believe in gravity. My actions *always* reflect my belief in gravity. I don't always *think* about gravity, but my belief in gravity dictates the way I think about the world; I don't act against it. And by the way—my belief in gravity *saves* me. It keeps me from stepping off cliffs.

Belief is best understood as the readiness to act as if what I believe is really true. What I do—my "works"—reveals what it is I *really* believe, my mental map about how things are.

This is why Jesus' brother James speaks about faith the way he does:

> What good is it, my brothers and sisters, if someone claims to have faith but has no deeds? Can such faith save them? Suppose a brother or a sister is without clothes and daily food. If one of you says to them, "Go in peace; keep warm and well fed," but does nothing about their physical needs, what good is it? In the same way, faith by itself, if it is not accompanied by action, is dead.
>
> JAMES 2:14-17

This passage has created huge controversy. Some people respond, "I thought all I had to do was believe the right stuff." Some people think James is disagreeing with Paul, who said we are saved by faith alone. James is simply pointing out that our actions inevitably reveal our mental map—our faith—about how things are.

James asks about people who claim to have faith but don't care for the poor, "Can such faith save them?" (James 2:14). If you've been around churches much, you know that "saving faith" is a really important Bible idea. But many people in churches, whether they know it or not, define saving faith as "the bare minimum amount I have to believe such that if I believe it, God has to let me into heaven when I die."

But we're not called to believe the minimum amount. We're called to have the faith *of* Jesus, Jesus' mental map about the way things are.

To have saving faith is not to believe the minimum amount so God has to let you in. To have saving faith is to believe what Jesus himself believed, to see what Jesus himself saw, so that you naturally do what Jesus himself would do.

Earlier James puts it like this: "Don't combine the faith *of* our Lord Jesus Christ with favoritism" (see James 2:1). This is, again, sometimes translated "faith *in* Jesus." But it's most naturally translated the "faith *of* Jesus." This saving faith includes a gloriously transformed Reticular Activating System that notices and delights in people as beloved image bearers of God regardless of wealth or color or beauty or youth or power; that notices pockets of poverty and neighborhoods of need and asks, "God, how can I help?" more than pockets of affluence and neighborhoods of wealth and asks, "God, how can I get?"

"Saving faith" is not just good news for the one who has it. It's good news for the poor; it's good news for orphans and widows; it's good news for the trafficked; it's good news for the bullied; it's good news for the hungry; it's good news for the refugee.

Saving faith is what makes people say, "Here's my time; I'll serve"; "Here's my money; I'll give"; "Here's my life; I'll care."

Because having a loving Father watching over them and over every member of the human race has gone from a creed they profess to their mental map of the way things are. They believe it like gravity. And it doesn't just save them; it becomes a part of God's project to save the world. This is illumination: our coming, as disciples, to have the faith of Jesus Christ, to believe what Jesus believed, so that it changes our mental map, so that we begin to live as Jesus lived. He was called "the true light" (John 1:9); saving faith enables our lights to so shine that others see our good deeds and glorify our father in heaven (see Matthew 5:16).

RISE AND SHINE

It is to produce this faith as a mental map that causes the teacher to bring his students to the water of Caesarea Philippi. He is not trying to create people who profess things *about* him. He's trying to create children of light.

So let's return to Jesus' pop quiz. Jesus had just asked the million-dollar question: "Who do you say I am?" While the answers came easily before, now only one responds.

> Simon Peter answered, "You are the Christ, the Son of the living God."
>
> Jesus replied, "Blessed are you, Simon son of Jonah, for this was not revealed to you by man, but by my Father in heaven. And I tell you that you are Peter, and on this rock I will build my church, and the gates of Hades will not overcome it. I will give you the keys of the kingdom of heaven; whatever you bind on earth will be bound in heaven, and whatever you loose on earth will be loosed in heaven."
>
> MATTHEW 16:16-19

Imagine how Peter felt. "I got an A! If any of you guys want a little tutoring on this discipleship thing, I'm available after class."

What was Peter saying? "You're the Christ." Some people think "Christ" is Jesus' last name, like he's from the Christ family. But *Christ* is the Greek word for the Messiah, the Anointed One.

"You are . . . the Son of the living God." There were lots of other gods. Look around the grotto—they had lots of sons. But none of them was alive.

There was still a *lot* that Peter didn't understand. Here's what he got: "You're *it*. You're what the world has been waiting for. You're the *one*."

The light has dawned.

There's a wonderful translation of this passage in the Hawaiian Pidgin version: "Simon Peter say, 'You da Christ Guy, da Spesho Guy God Wen Send. Da God who alive fo real kine, you his Boy.'"[5]

Jesus doesn't say, "Simon, you are right." Jesus says, "You are *blessed*." Interesting response. Usually in school if you get the answer right, the teacher doesn't say, "Blessed are you, Charley."

Blessed is an important Jesus word. He uses it in the Sermon on the Mount in what is known as the Beatitudes. "Blessed are the poor in Spirit. . . . Blessed are those who mourn. . . . Blessed are the meek . . . " (see Matthew 5:3-12). The blessed are those for whom the Kingdom of God—life in God's presence and power and forgiveness and love—is now available. Through Jesus.

And the reason knowing what Peter knows about Jesus matters so much is now you don't have to wonder if what Jesus says is true. You don't have to wonder about the right path to follow. You can live together with your friend Jesus in growing confidence and light in his Kingdom.

You have a new identity in him. In Greek, the word for Peter—*petros*—means "rock." "You're not unstable, impulsive Simon anymore. You're Rocky."

You have a new authority. "Here are the keys. Got 'em from my dad. You can go on in. You can help others in. You have a new mission."

You have a new assurance. "The Gates of Hades will not prevail. They're right over there. I'm going to the realm of the dead, but I'm coming back. You don't even have to worry about dying."

In illumination, the reality of a new world opens up to me at the deepest level of my being, a level far deeper than we normally associate with religious beliefs.

You'd think that would be the end of the story, but it's not. This is a quiz with two parts.

With Jesus, the quiz always has two parts.

From that time on Jesus began to explain to his
disciples that he must go to Jerusalem and suffer many
things at the hands of the elders, the chief priests and
the teachers of the law, and that he must be killed.
MATTHEW 16:21

This is very strange to them. This is not in the script.

Peter says, "Boys, I got this. I just got an A in Messiahology. I'll straighten this out."

"Peter took him aside and began to rebuke him. 'Never, Lord!' he said. 'This shall never happen to you!'" (Matthew 16:22).

"Peter took him aside." Imagine this: "Look, Lord, I don't

want to embarrass you in front of the fellas. But you've got to stop this negative thinking, or the guys are gonna get discouraged. I didn't just become pope for this! Our side's gonna win; their side's gonna lose."

But Jesus responds, "Get behind me, Satan. You are a stumbling block to me; you do not have in mind the concerns of God, but merely human concerns" (Matthew 16:23).

Peter says, "I liked that other nickname—'Rocky'—better. Could we ix-nay on the atan-Say?"

Peter's head has got to be spinning now. "You're my rock—I'm going to build on you. You're Satan—get behind me."

Jesus' main vehicle on earth is going to be the church.

Jesus' main problem on earth is going to be the church.

You can get the right answers and still become the wrong person. Jesus' own brother James wrote, "You believe that there is one God. Good! Even the demons believe that—and shudder" (James 2:19).

Illumination is about more than being able to give the right answer. Illumination is being able to *see*. For Helen Keller, it was the moment when she suddenly connected the touch of her teacher with the feel of the water. "I see it now! I understand!"—and a new world of meaning opened up.

Illumination is the new mental map that comes to Jesus' disciples. During Jesus' life, and even more after his death and resurrection, his disciples experienced this in continually new and thrilling ways: "I see—God loves even the Samaritans."

"I see—it really is more blessed to give than to receive." "I see with the loaves and fish—little is much when God is in it." "I see when I get out of the boat—my God is stronger than the storm." "I see when sent to the Roman centurion Cornelius—with God there truly are no favorites."

Illumination comes to us through obedience. Correct information is necessary but not sufficient. I may *affirm* the goodness of generosity, but it's only when I actually, repeatedly give—and experience the joy and strength that goes with giving, and watch as God's provision to me becomes more apparent, and notice how gratitude emerges more often when I'm generous than when I'm hoarding—that I receive *illumination*.

Illumination comes to us through obedience. That's why Jesus goes on to say to his disciples, "If anyone would come after me, he must deny himself and take up his cross and follow me. For whoever wants to save his life will lose it, but whoever loses his life for me will find it" (Matthew 16:24-25).

Jesus doesn't want people whose main goal and identity is that they give the right religious answers. Those are the people who are going to kill him.

He doesn't want answer givers; he wants life givers. Illumination itself has an inside and an outside dimension. My mind is enlightened. But the result is that my life becomes a source of light to others, as Miss Sullivan was to Helen Keller, and in turn Helen Keller became to countless others living in the dark.

This "outside" dimension of illumination is celebrated by Isaiah:

> Arise, shine, for your light has come,
>   and the glory of the LORD rises upon you.
> See, darkness covers the earth
>   and thick darkness is over the peoples,
> but the LORD rises upon you
>   and his glory appears over you.
> Nations will come to your light,
>   and kings to the brightness of your dawn. . . .
> Then you will look and be radiant.
>
> ISAIAH 60:1-5

Arise (awaken). Shine. How do we do that?

Jesus said, "You are the light of the world. . . . Let your light shine before others, that they may see your good deeds and glorify your Father in heaven" (Matthew 5:14-16).

We're in school to become children of light. Our goal is not to try harder to do good things. Through being open to the Holy Spirit; through wise use of spiritual practices that make space for God to interrupt our normal darkened thoughts and desires and exchanging them for truth-filled thoughts and noble desires; through relationships with those inside Jesus' community and outside, we seek to become children of light. "For you were once darkness, but now you are light in the Lord. Live as children of light (for the fruit of the light consists in all goodness, righteousness and truth)" (Ephesians 5:8-9).

"Who do you say that I am?" The question remains. It turns out that Jesus is "the living word that awakened their souls; that gave them light, joy, and hope; that set them free." The most important day of their lives was when the Teacher came to them. That day connected two eras of immeasurable contrast, filling them with wonder.

Not just them. The very calendar we use is divided into two eras, based on the day he came. "The true light that gives light to everyone was coming into the world" (John 1:9).

And yet our need for more light and new learning never ends. Jesus our Teacher will be enlightening us as long as we live, just as he did for his first disciples.

Jesus' last pop quiz was given the night before he died. Jesus asks, "Who's the foot washer?"

The disciples say, "I don't know."

"It's me. In the Kingdom, greatness is servanthood."

The water is poured.

The light dawns.

"Take off your sandals. There's John's feet. Andrew's feet. Simon, there's yours. I know you by your feet."

UNION
Never Alone

I have been crucified with Christ and
I no longer live, but Christ lives in me.

GALATIANS 2:20

It is Peter's last intimate conversation with his friend Jesus.

The Crucifixion is past. Peter's denial of Jesus—uttered not just once but three times—is a horrible memory. The Resurrection has occurred, leading to joy and fear and confusion.

Peter and the disciples go fishing out on the lake. The text deliberately tells us it is Peter's idea. Maybe Peter has decided that, even though the Resurrection has occurred, his failure is too great, his destiny is lost, his separation from Jesus is irrevocable, and he will go back to his old identity and vocation. What goes around comes around.

A stranger stands on the shore. He asks if the disciples have caught any fish. Not a single one, they tell him. He instructs them to throw their nets on the right side of the boat. They do, and the haul of fish is so great that their nets can't hold them and begin to break. John is the first to realize it: the divine Fish Finder is at it again. What goes around comes around.

On the first performance of this miracle, Peter sank to his knees and asked Jesus to go away. This time he cannot wait to get close. With his trademark impulsiveness, Peter leaps into the water with his clothes on and outswims the boat to Jesus.

When Peter gets to the shore, Jesus is before a charcoal fire, cooking fish and baking bread for breakfast. It was in front of a charcoal fire that Peter denied Jesus three times. The sense of smell is said to evoke emotional memory more powerfully than any of our other senses.[1] It is not accidental that Jesus starts such a fire, or that the Gospel of John includes this detail. Peter is reminded of his estrangement from his friend.

After breakfast Jesus speaks to Peter. He addresses him formally: "Simon son of John." Jesus does not use his old familiar nickname—Peter, the "Rock"; not even just Simon—but "Simon son of John," the way we do when a relationship has experienced a breach. Peter must have wondered in that moment if his old intimacy with Jesus was now lost.

"Simon son of John, do you love me more than these?" (John 21:15).

It is an achingly vulnerable question. In *Fiddler on the Roof,* the main character, Tevye, sits shyly with his wife, Golde, wondering at the strange new world in which their daughter marries a man not because of a matchmaker's order but simply because of love. A question occurs to him. With uncharacteristic bashfulness he asks her, "Golde—do you love me?"

"Do I *what*?"

He asks again. She evades. Eventually, in a charming song, they realize they love each other. "It doesn't change a thing, but even so, after twenty-five years, it's nice to know."

It doesn't change a thing.

Except that it changes *everything*.

Can a human being love God? Can a person be on intimate terms with the divine? Can a mortal being experience union with the infinite?

I wonder if Jesus was shy when he asked Peter this question, a little bit like an adolescent, a little bit like a parent with an estranged child, a little bit like Tevye with Golde. "Peter, do you love me?"

"Yes, Lord," Peter answers.

For reasons Peter must have wondered about, Jesus asks him again. "Simon son of John, do you love me?"

Again, Peter answers, "Yes, Lord, you know that I love you" (John 21:16).

And then a third time. At first Peter is hurt. Does Jesus not believe him? "Lord, you know all things; you know that I love you" (John 21:17).

And they speak more about Peter's future, about what he will suffer, about how God will use Peter's sufferings just as God has used Jesus' sufferings.

And Peter remembers, if not at that moment, then later on. Three times, before a charcoal fire, he had the chance to express his love for Jesus and instead denied him.

Crucifixion. Agony.

Resurrection. Hope.

Three times, before a charcoal fire, he has the chance to express his love for Jesus. And this time he gets it right.

What goes around comes around.

And then Jesus says to him, one more time, at the end of their time together, what he said to him the first time—"Follow me" (John 21:19)—showing, perhaps, that in the spiritual life, we're never really done. As long as we're alive, the journey toward Jesus is never finished—we awaken and need purging and get illumined and experience oneness and need awakening all over again someplace else.

What goes around comes around.

But what we are moving toward, in our coming and our going, in the strange, spiraling, three-steps-forward, two-steps-backward pilgrimage, is something so transcendently great that it almost makes us blush to say the words.

Union with God.

"Do you love me?"

Peter will not see Jesus much after this encounter, but he will know a new and greater closeness to him, as though he is not just *with* Christ but *in* Christ.

Or that Christ is in him.

ABIDE IN ME

One of the founding moments of Alcoholics Anonymous involved a psychiatric patient of Carl Jung who thought he'd been healed and found himself drunk on the ship that was returning him to America. Jung wrote about this profound craving in a letter that became famous: "His (Roland W.'s) craving for alcohol was the low-level equivalent of the spiritual thirst of our being for wholeness, expressed in medieval language: the union with God."[2] It is perhaps not a coincidence that the Latin word for alcohol is *spiritus*, a word also used to refer to God. Even in English we'll sometimes call alcohol "spirits." Alcohol promises to remove the pain of loneliness. It magically makes people feel connected to their fellows and to life itself. It works—until it doesn't. It's hard to get enough of something that almost works.

"Let anyone who is thirsty come to me and drink," Jesus once said (John 7:37). "By this he meant the Spirit," John tells us (verse 39). All of us thirst for the Spirit. All of us thirst for union with God.

On his last night with his friends, Jesus taught them about living in union with God, a teaching that has lasted two thousand years.

This teaching consists of one metaphor—one picture—and one invitation. The picture is this: "I am the vine, you are the branches." The invitation is "Abide in me."

If you understand the picture, if you accept the invitation with the best wisdom and diligence you can give it, then Jesus says you can experience union with God.

Life itself is only possible through abiding. This is from Nobel Prize–winning physicist Erwin Schrödinger:

> What is the characteristic feature of life? When is a piece of matter said to be alive? When it goes on "doing something," moving, exchanging material with its environment, and so forth, and that for a much longer period than we would expect an inanimate piece of matter to "keep going" under similar circumstances.[3]

Put a pebble in the ground and nothing happens. Put a seed in the ground, and something in the ground says to something in the seed, "Put out a root," and it does, and the seed draws nourishment—life—from the soil. Something above the earth says to something in the seed, "Come on up," and that little seed sends up a vine from below the earth to above the earth, and eventually it's not just a seed anymore.

Here's the best definition of life that I know: Life is the "ability to contact and selectively take in from the surroundings whatever supports its own survival, extension, and enhancement."[4]

In other words, a living thing has a power inside it to interact with what lies beyond it and to draw from that beyond those things that can enhance it and grow it and make it fruitful.

When it comes to human beings, that need and capacity to interact with what lies beyond us is not just physical. We have a need for food, water, and sleep, but we also have a need for meaning and to love and be loved. Without this, our spirits shrivel up and die like a vine with no water. This is what it means to live, to abide: to draw nourishment from what is around us.

When we abide, we make a home (our "abode") in a place. We linger there, and our inner person gets shaped by our abode. We can abide in fear. We can abide in ambition. We can abide in anger. We can abide in lust.

Or we can abide in God.

The place where we abide is called "home." Home is where we have a sense of belonging and safety and being wanted. But home ends up being more than just walls.

When Nancy and I lived in the Midwest, we were talking to an elderly couple, Max and Esther, who had lived their whole lives in a really cold place. I asked them, "You could live anywhere—why do you live here?"

Max immediately touched his wife on the arm and said, "My home is wherever Esther is."

In the same talk where Jesus instructs his disciples to "abide in me," he tells them, "Anyone who loves me will obey my teaching" (John 14:23). It is in union with Christ—in our "abiding"—that obedience to Jesus becomes a dance of grace. It is in union that word becomes connected with touch. Union with God is not simply feeling God's closeness. It is having my will united with his will in surrender.

Jesus goes on to say, "My Father will love them, and we will come to them and make our home with them" (John 14:23). In love comes obedience, and in obedience comes "home." God wants to make your heart his home. God wants to make his heart your home.

In other words, God will save us from the loneliness that Mother Teresa called the epidemic of the modern world. But salvation is never just salvation *from*. It is always also salvation *for*. And the depth of the pain of our loneliness is an indicator of the height of the union for which we were made.

We are tempted to believe that other people can save us from our loneliness. In an old movie a blonde is locked in a tight embrace with Groucho Marx, demanding of him, "Hold me closer . . . closer." Groucho looks confused. "If I hold you any closer, I'd be in back of you." Bodies can touch bodies, but mere physical touch cannot remove the loneliness of the soul.

Soter ("savior") was a common term in the classical world. It was often used for a military figure or healer or king who bore the hopes of the people. Lots of people had that title. But not in the New Testament. It is used eight times of God and sixteen times of Jesus and of *nobody else*.[5] "Salvation belongs to our God, who sits on the throne, and to the Lamb" (Revelation 7:10).

This is because, as much as we look for deliverance from

our outward circumstances, the main task of salvation is an inside job. We must be saved from what's going on *inside*. And so far as I know, no other candidate for *soter* ever said, "Abide in me."

Caesar never said that.

Alexander the Great never said that.

Jesus said that.

Union with Christ—to abide with him—means that he is present in our minds and can communicate thoughts to us at any moment. Human beings are, more than anything else, minds—a ceaseless flow of awareness. Our minds are crucial because it is through our minds that we contact reality. When you hit your thumb with a hammer, you are mindful of it. Our greatest freedom is the freedom to direct what we think of. To be constantly mindful of God is salvation from worry, fear, and regret.

Union with Christ means he is present to my will, and I can surrender to him all day long. "I have been crucified with Christ," Paul says (Galatians 2:20). It is a key mark of the will that surrender is the one act of the will that never exhausts but always refreshes us. The will was made to surrender to God because we were made for union with God.

Rankin Wilbourne writes, "Christ dwelling in us by his Spirit is a guarantee that we can and will change."[6] John Calvin wrote that the possibility of union with Christ is why a mere belief in the atonement is not enough: "As long as Christ remains outside of us, and we are separated from him, all that he has suffered and done for the salvation of the human race remains useless and of no value to us."[7]

In order to understand what union is, it's helpful to know what it is not. Union does not mean the extinguishing of the self, and it does not mean the gratification of the self.

Union with God is not the loss of self; it does not mean that your self ceases to exist. In Huston Smith's *The World's Religions*, he notes that an observation of the Buddha that often startles people is that there is no such thing as soul, that the "self" is an illusion.[8] The "union" of the self with the infinite in such traditions is sometimes described using the analogy of a glass of water being poured into the ocean; it has not ceased to exist but has totally merged with something vastly larger.

The problem with this image is that the drops in a glass of water were there coincidentally; they had no identity and no character. No one names their glass of water. In the Christian tradition, however, a person is a unique and indivisible center of consciousness with a will and an identity. I have three children, and I want them to be close to each other, but if I had them fused into a single splendid being, I would be in great trouble with my wife. It is the separateness of my self that allows me to offer myself in continual service and love to God.

Union with God does not mean passivity, or having no desires, or effortless bliss. On the other hand, our destiny is not the gratification of the self. Writer Ayn Rand spoke of the "triumph of the will"; she celebrated the courageous individualist who above all else imposed her or his will on every situation. Far from wanting to merge with others, in this view, our calling is the "will to power" without sentiment or weakness. (My daughter once wrote a satirical article featuring Ayn Rand reviewing children's movies. Her faux review of *Old Yeller*: "A farm animal ceases to be useful and is disposed of humanely. A valuable lesson for children.—*Four stars*."[9])

Our problem when we seek union with someone else and seek to gratify our own self is, whose will is going to win? A couple gets married and the minister says, "The two shall become one"—but *which* one? I want it to be *me*. Union with God does not mean that I will get whatever I want. It does not mean the world will bend to my will. It is not the same as being in a constantly good mood.

what its not

PARTICIPATION IN CHRIST

As we've seen, union is not the loss of the self. And it's not the gratification of the self. Rather, it is the participation of the self in the life of God.

When you enter the Church of the Resurrection in Kansas City, you are immediately overwhelmed by the largest stained-glass window built this century. The window is dominated by images of three gardens. The church's pastor Adam Hamilton says that the story of salvation can be told by these three gardens.

The first is the Garden of Eden, where we were invited into union with God and where union was lost.

On the far right is the garden described at the end of the Bible, where the tree of life grows leaves used "for the healing of the nations" (Revelation 22:2). Union restored.

In the middle is the garden of Gethsemane, where Jesus experienced *dis*union from God so that we could be reunited with him.

When I was a boy, my grandmother, who lived with us, had a favorite old hymn called "In the Garden." She would sing it in her old-lady tremulous voice: "And he walks with me, and he talks with me, and he tells me I am his own . . ."

Even when that song was popular, it was often criticized for being sentimental, and I suppose it was, but it spoke to my grandmother. She had been a widow many years when she lived with us, and although she did not complain, you could hear the longing and ache in her voice when she sang that song. Salvation is a return to the Garden, a return to union.

We die in isolation. We thrive when we are connected. We were made for union with God.

This idea can sound esoteric or like an experience reserved for monks and mystics, but you have already tasted it: When you were so caught up in a moment of play, or music, or work, or creating, or relating that was so filled with life that you lost all concern for yourself and yet felt more yourself than ever. When you knew yourself to be not alone. When you were drawn toward being your best self. When you were overcome with gratitude or joy. When you were surrendered.

C. S. Lewis writes that not only do we long for beauty, we long for something else so deep, it can hardly be put into words—"to be united with the beauty we see, to pass into it, to receive it into ourselves, to bathe in it, to become part of it." Now we hardly ever taste such a thing. But "all the leaves of the New Testament are rustling with the rumor that it will not always be so. Some day, God willing, we shall get *in*."[10]

As we saw earlier, the apostle Paul never talks about how to become a Christian, but he does talk about being "in Christ" or about Christ being in us. A search of the New Testament turns up more than 150 instances of the phrase.[11] Where did this idea of being "in Christ" come from, and what does it mean? Richard Hays writes that the foundation of Paul's thought was not some abstract doctrine but the very narrative of the gospel story about Jesus. "Paul's readers have come to *participate* in the story of Jesus."[12]

Klyne Snodgrass puts it like this: "In Paul's understanding, Christian identity derives from being in Christ, from participation in Christ. . . . Participation is *the* essential ingredient in Christianity."[13]

Paul experienced this participation so deeply that he could say things like "I am no longer living, but Christ lives in me" (Galatians 2:20). Martin Luther said, "You are so cemented to Christ that He and you are as one person, which cannot be separated but remains attached to him forever." His wife, Katharina, put it more simply when she said on her deathbed, "I will stick to Christ as a burr to a cloth."

Salvation means participation in Christ.

There is a difference between merely *living* in a country that is a democracy and *participating* in democracy. Participation means action: I read, I learn, I act, I vote, I write, I volunteer.

There is a difference between attending a dance and dancing. Participation means action: I risk, I ask, I move, I rhumba or twist or waltz or moonwalk or Macarena or twerk.

Miroslav Volf notes that we have a "wrongly centered self that needs to be de-centered by being nailed to a cross."[14] To participate in Christ means that my ego and will have received a new center so that my experience of daily life becomes changed. It is not passive on my part. It is full of action. I invite him, I ask, I pray, I learn, I thank, I give. I engage in practices that make space for God. However, these practices, contrary to what many think, are not the primary expression of participation with God. They are a "means of grace," vehicles through which I receive power and freedom so that the ordinary moments of my ordinary life can be an exercise in participation in Christ. I am inspired, encouraged, guided, convicted, strengthened, and made confident in my working and playing and relating. I die to fear and pride and misguided desire so that I can live in love and joy and peace.

THE VINE AND THE BRANCHES

Let's return to Jesus' picture of the vine and the branches. Jesus tells his disciples,

> Abide in me as I abide in you. Just as the branch cannot bear fruit by itself unless it abides in the vine, neither can you unless you abide in me. I am the vine; you are the branches. Those who abide in me and I in them bear much fruit, because apart from me you can do nothing.
>
> JOHN 15:4-5, NRSV

This is where most people get God wrong.

The branch's job is not to produce fruit. The branch's job is to continually receive life from the vine—to abide. The fruit is a by-product of abiding.

The branch is you and me. (Just as banks have branch offices, so does the Kingdom of God—and that's us!) The fruit is the external manifestation of what's going on inside the branch. It's our behavior. It's the things we do and say all day long.

People think, *God's up there, and in addition to all the other stuff I have to do every day, I have to do some things to keep God happy. I have to go to church. I have to give some money. I have to read the Bible. And I have to avoid some things. I have to avoid stealing. I have to avoid lying—unless I'm really, really in trouble. I have to avoid saying bad words—especially when I'm in church.*

But their inner dimension of heart and personality—the inside of the branch—remains untransformed. They don't love. They don't even *know* they don't love because they're too busy trying to produce fruit.

Then people will think, *This takes effort. It means giving up a lot of good stuff. I sure hope God is real so I get rewarded for this some day.* This has the tendency to make religious people judgmental toward nonreligious people. *They get to party on Saturday night and sleep in on Sunday. No fair.*

Jesus knows exactly how this works. Jesus tells a story about a wayward son, and his older brother is the picture of a religious person. Jesus says the wayward son "set off for a distant country and there squandered his wealth in wild living" (Luke 15:13).

The older brother is filled with judgment and superiority and is furious with his father when the father welcomes the wayward brother back. Here's what the older brother says: "When this son of yours who has squandered your property with prostitutes comes home, you kill the fattened calf for him!" (Luke 15:30).

The interesting thing is that Jesus' story doesn't say anything about prostitutes. Where does the older brother get that idea? Most likely his thoughts run like this: *Oh, my foolish younger brother. Breaking my father's heart. Squandering his money. I wonder how he's spending it. Probably on sex. That's what I'd do if I thought I could get away with it. If I'm going to miss out on the good stuff, I better get commended for my moral superiority, and I better get eternally compensated.*

That's what's going on in the older brother's branch.

What's going on inside the branch is that stream of ceaseless thoughts and feelings and desires and perceptions and intentions that just seem automatic. And the "fruit" is the external manifestation—words and actions and habits—that *reveal* what's going on inside the branch. The great problem religious people have is they think God is way out there somewhere and they have to try as hard as they can to produce fruit—to say and do the right thing—to please this impossible-to-please God.

But you will never produce the right fruit by trying to produce the right fruit.

You will never say and do the right thing by trying to say and do the right thing.

You will never obey the law by trying to obey the law.

You will never do the right actions by trying to do the right actions.

The inside of the branch must change. The automatic flow of thoughts and desires and intentions must change from being ego centered and conflicted and greedy and fearful to confident and grateful and humble and joyful and ready to love.

How does that happen?

"I am the vine; you are the branches. Abide in me . . ."

Jesus means this in a literal sense. C. S. Lewis writes, "When Christians say the Christ-life is in them, they do not mean simply something mental or moral. . . . This is not simply a way of saying that they are thinking about Christ or copying Him.

They mean that Christ is actually operating through them; that the whole mass of Christians are the physical organism through which Christ acts—that we are His fingers and muscles, the cells of His body."[15]

Practically speaking, how do I pursue this?

I abandon myself, mind and will, to God.

Primarily, it involves that ceaseless flow of conscious experience that lies at the heart of intimacy. We consist of our conscious experiences—our awareness and thoughts from one moment to the next. Just like the roots of a seed reach out to take in something from beyond it, our thoughts are constantly reaching out and taking in things from beyond us—for better or worse, wisely or foolishly.

This is why Paul says,

Whatever is true, whatever is noble, whatever is
right, whatever is pure, whatever is lovely, whatever is
admirable—if anything is excellent or praiseworthy—
think about such things. Whatever you have learned or
received or heard from me, or seen in me—put it into
practice. And the God of peace will be with you.
PHILIPPIANS 4:8-9

This is life on the vine. This is what salvation looks like.

Apart from the vine, my mind takes in worry and discontentment. My friend Santiago, who got his MBA from Harvard, said his professor would ask them about each business they studied by saying, "Who's winning today: greed or fear?" Those were the only two choices. Those are the predominant thoughts of the human mind disconnected from God: "I want"; "I'm afraid." When I'm off the vine, my thoughts are like anchors. They weigh me down constantly. Am I successful? Why doesn't X like me? What if I need more money?

what are my thoughts?

On the vine, we take in God's thoughts, God's life. Greed and fear are replaced by gratitude and confidence—gratitude for God's goodness and affection; confidence in his presence and strength.

This is why the first psalm says,

Blessed is the one . . .
whose delight is in the law of the LORD,
    and who meditates on his law day and night.
That person is like a tree planted by streams of water,
    which yields its fruit in season
and whose leaf does not wither—
    whatever they do prospers.

PSALM 1:1-3

Years ago we got a little orange tree for our first house. The scent of orange blossoms is my favorite California smell. I planted it, watered it, fertilized it, put Miracle-Gro on it. I loved that tree.

One week when we were gone, our six-year-old neighbor came and dug up all the tree's roots. When we got home, our tree was dead.

Why? Because the health of the roots is the health of the tree. Without good roots, there is no fruit.

Our thoughts are the roots of our spirit. Our job is not to try to generate more God-pleasing actions by greater willpower. Our job is to abide—to be rooted in Christ.

This is what Jesus gets at when he says, "If you abide in me, and my words abide in you . . ." (John 15:7, NRSV). Often we are tempted to turn that into a burden: *Now in addition to everything else I have to do, I'm supposed to memorize Scripture verses or else God won't be happy with me.*

But words will *inevitably* abide in us. The words that abide in us are simply the thoughts that flow through our minds. They can be good or bad. We may choose them intentionally or allow them to dwell haphazardly. But one truth is certain: we are formed by the words that abide in us.

So Jesus is not really calling us to do something in addition to what we already do. He's calling us to do what we already do in a different way: to seek to have *his* words be the ones abiding in our minds.

This is what it means to be *with* someone. When we're with another person, they are the one most present in our thoughts. When we are present with another person, we *think* of them— think of what they've said, how we know them. Their bodily presence and facial expression and voice guide our thoughts. Even if our bodies are separated, we can speak with someone over the phone or Skype with them and see their faces. With memory, we can in a sense abide with those who are no longer living.

But because Jesus is present on earth through his Spirit, without limitation of body, he is *really* and *literally* able to communicate and commune directly with us. And this moment-by-moment communion with us is what allows us to obey him:

> As the Father has loved me, so I have loved you; abide in my love. If you keep my commandments, you will abide in my love, just as I have kept my Father's commandments and abide in his love. I have said these things to you so that my joy may be in you, and that your joy may be complete.
>
> This is my commandment, that you love one another as I have loved you. No one has greater love than this, to lay down one's life for one's friends. You are my friends if you do what I command you. I do not call you servants any longer, because the servant does not know what the master is doing; but I have called you friends, because I have made known to you everything that I have heard from my Father.
>
> JOHN 15:9-15, NRSV

"You are my friends if you do what I command you." Imagine: What might it be like to live as a friend of Jesus for a day?

You might start first thing in the morning. If you're not a morning person, if no one wants to be around you until you've had your coffee—if even *Jesus* doesn't want to be around you until you've had your coffee—get your coffee first. Coffee is from Jesus too. ("I am the vine; you are the bean.")

Then, take the Lord's Prayer. Walk through it one phrase at a time.

"Our Father." Think of the tenderest picture of father love you know, and bask in the thought that your heavenly Father loves you. Sit with it.

"Hallowed be your name." *Help me and everyone else today realize what a wonderful person you are.*

"Your kingdom come, your will be done on earth as it is in heaven." *I'm perfectly safe all day because I'm in your kingdom, and your kingdom is never in trouble, and neither are those in it.*

Invoke God's presence. Walk through your plans for the day with God, and invite him to be with you. Form the conscious intention *Today I will abide on the vine.*

But I am imperfect, you might think, *and my rival kingdom is strong. What do I do when I get it wrong? What do I do when I disobey for the thousandth time, or I worry, or I lust, or I lie, or I yell at my kids, or I get drunk, or I betray my closest friend?*

Get back on the vine.

The vine isn't going anywhere. The vine is very patient. The vine will never say, "You stupid branch. I'm so tired of your poor performance. Don't even think about coming back."

George Carlin used to talk about the difference between how you score points in football and how you score points in baseball. Football is a violent effort: you attack your enemies by throwing bombs and engaging in a ground attack until you soften up their defenses and make it to the end zone.

In baseball, there's no battle. You just come home.

With the Father, it's much more like baseball than like football. It's not a grueling battle. As with the Prodigal Son in Jesus' story, you come to your senses in the far country. You just come home. The Father is always waiting.

THE LORD OF THE DANCE

Union with God is all a gift of grace. It is a response to his love and acceptance and invitation and abundant goodness.

Some time ago my wife, who is a lovely dancer, asked me if I would take dance lessons so we could dance together. I was not sure. My people are not a dancing people. But I love my wife, and it was clear that there would be many advantages to doing this, so I said yes.

We went to the studio and were given a little book that had pictures of footsteps placed appropriately for waltz and fox-trot and rhumba. This was good. I'm good with books. I can deal with books.

I read the book.

I knew the book.

I could even *do* the book.

But there was no grace. Picture, if you've seen *Young Frankenstein*, Peter Boyle as the Monster lumbering to "Puttin' on the Ritz," and that's me. On a good day. The secret of a body in motion, the ability to flow effortlessly to music, was not present, to say the least.

Then I asked my wife to dance. She has grace. She grew up dancing and has a way of moving with fluidity and joy that has always been beautiful to me.

And the strangest thing happened. A little of her grace spilled over into me. Only a little, but it was enough to keep me dancing and to make me hunger for more. I began to move with more grace when I was dancing with her than I ever experienced on my own.

Dancing is about more than knowing the book and doing the book. In a dance, the partners are no longer separate. They know each other, adjust to each other, delight in each other, accommodate each other.

Many centuries ago the church fathers and mothers used the term *perichoresis* to describe the Trinity. *Peri-* means "around" (think of a perimeter); *chorein* means to move or to make room for. The picture is of a kind of divine rotation. While sin causes us to want the world to revolve around us, within the Godhead there is a kind of decentering: the Father and Son and Holy

Spirit make room for, move toward, and circle one another with love. The word is so lovely that over time it came to suggest a kind of "circle dance" of the Trinity, where the delight in serving and loving so fills the members of the Trinity that dance is the only adequate picture.

We were made to be united with God because God himself is a union of three persons in perfect oneness. In *Mere Christianity*, C. S. Lewis describes the union of the Trinity as "almost, if you will not think me irreverent, a kind of dance. The union between the Father and the Son is such a live concrete thing that this union itself is also a Person. . . . Each one of us has got to enter that pattern, take his place in that dance. There is no other way to the happiness for which we were made."[16]

Jesus spoke once about how people neither responded to John the Baptist's austerity ("We sang a dirge, and you did not cry") nor to his own party-going, sinner-accepting, life-giving joy ("We played the flute for you, and you did not dance," Luke 7:32).

That's Jesus on the flute. In the memorable words of Edward Schillebeeckx, "Being sad in Jesus' presence was an existential impossibility."[17] You gotta dance.

There is a Christmas carol about Jesus that is hundreds of years old called "Tomorrow Shall Be My Dancing Day." In it, Jesus, the "Lord of the Dance," sings,

Tomorrow shall be my dancing day;
I would my true love did so chance

To see the legend of my play,
To call my true love to my dance.

We were made to dance.

When the dance is done right, you can hardly tell where one person stops and the other starts. They have become one. And yet each feels more fully themselves than ever.

Just as there's a physical reality, so there is a spiritual reality. That reality can provide you with love and security and confidence and sufficiency and contentment and gratitude and peace and joy.

This is wonderful, and union is a great gift to us, but it never comes solely for *us*. In union with God, the default mode of my will becomes to bless. The will that is disconnected from God constantly seeks what it wants. The will that is "on the vine" constantly moves outward in blessing. In union we learn to bless constantly—bless the e-mails we write (we'll write them better), bless the brownies we bake (they'll taste better), bless other drivers on the road. (They'll drive better. Probably. For sure you will.) Jesus prayed that we could know oneness with him and the Father "so that the world may believe" (John 17:21).

"If you remain in me and I in you, you will bear much fruit" (John 15:5). By abiding in Jesus, fruit—love, joy, peace, and so on—is the natural by-product. But fruit isn't for the branch's benefit. Fruit is the result of an overflow, an abundance of life. A vine bears fruit to spread the seeds of new life.

When Jesus restores Peter to union with him, he asks Peter three times to care for the sheep that Jesus loves.

Later, before he ascends to heaven, Jesus tells his disciples, "Surely I am with you always, to the very end of the age." And he gives them this command: "Go and make disciples of all nations, baptizing them in the name of the Father and of the Son and of the Holy Spirit, and teaching them to obey everything I have commanded you" (Matthew 28:19-20). The two go together.

Out of union, love flows. Jesus is calling his true love to the dance. And the invitation we receive becomes an invitation to others. What goes around comes around.

ACKNOWLEDGMENTS

I fondly hope this little book can help stimulate a fresh conversation about the glorious nature of salvation. I hope it can help people inside the church and out to see the indissoluble connection between the gospel Jesus preached and the discipleship he offered and to encourage people to "sell all they have in great joy" in order to follow him.

This project was inspired and made possible by Eff and Patty Martin, who helped to create a trip to Israel and a series of messages that formed the starting point of the book. Their generosity and warm enthusiasm for a true understanding of the gospel message of Jesus has impacted countless lives. Gary Moon is both a lifelong friend and a partner in thought, faith, and ministry, and we had many long conversations on both sides of the world about the matters discussed in this book.

Mark Nelson was generous with his time in a number of conversations that helped to bring clarity; a few of them delightfully included Tremper Longman III. Both Rich Mouw and Rankin Wilbourne were kind enough to read through the manuscript and offer feedback that was gratefully received. Laura Turner was a constant thought prodder, even while hatching other projects.

Tyndale has offered a wonderful team. Carol Traver and Jonathan Schindler were full of wisdom and encouragement and fun. They were also willing to hold lengthy conversations to help push these ideas to greater clarity and accessibility. Ron Beers is a constant source of ideas and possibilities; Jan Harris offered probing questions and numerous insights that enriched the manuscript.

I am most grateful to Menlo Church for making a life of ministry and studying and teaching and leading and writing possible. Linda Barker is the source of more joy than she knows. Sue Kim-Ahn and Eugene Lee and Jake Chacko are a team that anyone would pay money to be a part of.

Nancy has cheered on every writing project I've ever done. I suppose a conversation with her lies behind more words than I can imagine.

The life and thoughts and writings of Dallas Willard are simply never out of my mind as I think about the topics addressed here. I am indebted to him for the title on the cover of this book and much of whatever value lies inside it.

NOTES

INTRODUCTION: ARE WE THERE YET?

1. Bobby Azarian, "Apeirophobia: The Fear of Eternity," *Atlantic*, September 1, 2016, https://www.theatlantic.com/science/archive/2016/09/apeirophobia -the-fear-of-eternity/498368/.
2. Brenda B. Colijn, *Images of Salvation in the New Testament* (Downers Grove, IL: InterVarsity Press), 88.
3. Ibid., 96.
4. J. W. Roberts, quoted in Colijn, *Images of Salvation*.
5. Stephen Prothero, *God Is Not One* (HarperCollins, 2010), 65–66, 72–73.
6. See, for example, Ali Hasan and Richard Fumerton, "Knowledge by Acquaintance vs. Description," in *Stanford Encyclopedia of Philosophy*, March 10, 2014, https://plato.stanford.edu/entries/knowledge-acquaindescrip.
7. Dallas Willard, *Renewing the Christian Mind: Essays, Interviews, and Talks*, ed. Gary Black Jr. (New York: HarperOne, 2016), 307.
8. John Calvin quoted in Robert C. Roberts, *Spiritual Emotions: A Psychology of Christian Virtues* (Grand Rapids, MI: William B. Eerdmans, 2007), 157.
9. Dallas Willard, *The Spirit of the Disciplines: Understanding How God Changes Lives* (New York: HarperSanFrancisco, 1988), 32.
10. Huston Smith, *The Soul of Christianity: Restoring the Great Tradition* (New York: HarperCollins, 2005), 77.

CHAPTER 1: BREAKING NEWS

1. Dallas Willard, *Renovation of the Heart: Putting On the Character of Christ* (Colorado Springs, CO: NavPress, 2012), 108.
2. C. S. Lewis, *The Problem of Pain* (New York: HarperOne, 2001), 141.

3. John Henry Newman quoted in Cornelius Plantinga Jr., *Not the Way It's Supposed to Be: A Breviary of Sin* (Grand Rapids, MI: William B. Eerdmans, 1995), 37.

4. Fleming Rutledge arranges her magisterial work *The Crucifixion* around these two dynamics: sin is guilt for which atonement must be made, and sin is an alien power that must be overcome. See Fleming Rutledge, *The Crucifixion: Understanding the Death of Jesus Christ* (Grand Rapids, MI: Eerdmans, 2015), 189.

5. Dallas Willard, *The Divine Conspiracy: Rediscovering Our Hidden Life in God* (New York: HarperSanFrancisco, 1998), 302.

6. Lewis, *The Problem of Pain*, 130.

7. Matthew W. Bates, *Salvation by Allegiance Alone: Rethinking Faith, Works, and the Gospel of Jesus the King* (Grand Rapids, MI: Baker Academic, 2017), 51.

8. See, for example, Matthew 4:17; Mark 1:14-15. Jesus announces the Kingdom, teaches about life in the Kingdom, and heals because the Kingdom (the range of God's effective will) is what prophets called *shalom*. See also Luke 8:1; Luke 9:1-2. The disciples were on the same mission with the same message as Jesus. In Matthew 6:10, Jesus says we are to pray for the Kingdom to come, for God's "will [to] be done on earth as it is in heaven." In Matthew 6:33, Jesus says to "seek first his kingdom." In Matthew 13:44, Jesus describes the Kingdom as treasure in a field, worthy of selling all we have to possess. And in Acts 28:31, at the very end of the book, Paul is proclaiming the Kingdom.

9. Willard, *The Divine Conspiracy*, 21.

10. Dallas Willard, personal communication with the author. See also Willard, *The Divine Conspiracy*, 399.

11. Miroslav Volf, *Flourishing: Why We Need Religion in a Globalized World* (New Haven, CT: Yale University Press, 2015), 10–11.

12. Miroslav Volf, *Exclusion and Embrace: A Theological Exploration of Identity, Otherness, and Reconciliation* (Nashville: Abingdon, 1996), 298.

CHAPTER 2: THE MINIMUM ENTRANCE REQUIREMENTS

1. Langston Hughes, *The Big Sea* (New York: Hill and Wang, 1968), 18–19.

2. Ibid., 19–20.

3. Ibid., 20–21.

4. "Bible Lacking Sinner's Prayer Returned for Full Refund," *Babylon Bee*, August 16, 2016, http://babylonbee.com/news/bible-lacking-sinners -prayer-returned-full-refund/.

5. George MacDonald, "Wisdom to Live By" from *The Writings, Spiritual Vision, and Legacy of George MacDonald & Michael Phillips*, 2006, http://www .macdonaldphillips.com/fromtheheart.html.

6. Rankin Wilbourne, *Union with Christ: The Way to Know and Enjoy God* (Colorado Springs: David C. Cook, 2016).

7. George MacDonald, "Justice," *Literature Network*, http://www.online -literature.com/george-macdonald/unspoken-sermons/31/.

8. Fleming Rutledge, *The Crucifixion: Understanding the Death of Jesus Christ* (Grand Rapids, MI: Eerdmans, 2015), 122.

9. G. K. Chesterton, *The Everlasting Man* (London: Hodder & Stoughton, 1930), 60.

10. Frederick Dale Bruner, *Matthew: A Commentary*, vol. 1, *The Christbook: Matthew 1–12*, rev. ed. (Grand Rapids, MI: Wm. B. Eerdmans, 2004), 31.

11. William Faulkner, *As I Lay Dying: The Corrected Text* (New York: Vintage International, 1990), 176.

12. Aleksandr Solzhenitsyn, *The Gulag Archipelago*, volume 1 (New York: Harper & Row, 1976), 168.

13. Cornelius Plantinga Jr., "Sin: Not the Way It's Supposed to Be," Christ on Campus Initiative, 2010, http://tgc-documents.s3.amazonaws.com/cci/ Pantinga.pdf.

14. Patrick Ramsey, "Union and Communion," *Meet the Puritans* (blog), March 30, 2017, http://www.meetthepuritans.com/blog/union-and-communion.

CHAPTER 3: FOLLOW ME

1. Laura Hillenbrand, *Unbroken: A World War II Story of Survival, Resilience, and Redemption* (New York: Random House, 2010), 376.

2. Michael Burkhimer, *Lincoln's Christianity* (Yardley, PA: Westholme, 2007), xi.

3. Huston Smith, *The Soul of Christianity: Restoring the Great Tradition* (New York: HarperCollins, 2005), 84.

4. Dallas Willard, *The Spirit of the Disciplines: Understanding How God Changes Lives* (New York: HarperCollins, 1988), 258.

5. Dietrich Bonhoeffer, *The Cost of Discipleship* (New York: Touchstone, 1959), 51.

6. See Matthew 22:34-40; John 13:35.

7. Tim Harmon, "Who's In and Who's Out? Christianity and Bounded Sets vs. Centered Sets," *Transformed* (blog), January 17, 2014, https://www .westernseminary.edu/transformedblog/2014/01/17/whos-in-and-whos -out-christianity-and-bounded-sets-vs-centered-sets/.

8. See Joshua 2:1; Hebrews 11:31; James 2:25.

9. C. S. Lewis, *Mere Christianity* (New York: HarperCollins, 1980), 209–10.

10. Simon Sinek, "How Great Leaders Inspire Action," filmed September 2009, at TEDxPugetSound, video, 17:58, https://www.ted.com/talks/simon_sinek _how_great_leaders_inspire_action.

11. Bonhoeffer, *The Cost of Discipleship*, 46, 56.

INTERLUDE: THE GREAT JOURNEY

1. Dallas Willard, *The Divine Conspiracy: Rediscovering Our Hidden Life in God* (New York: HarperSanFrancisco, 1998), 275.

2. *Alcoholics Anonymous*, 4th ed. (New York: Alcoholics Anonymous World Services, 2001), 88.

3. Martin Luther, quoted in James Arne Nestingen, *Martin Luther: His Life and Teachings* (Eugene, OR: Wipf and Stock, 2004), 38.

4. Linda Stone, "Continuous Partial Attention," https://lindastone.net/qa /continuous-partial-attention/.

5. *Union* has been used in different ways by different writers. For instance, the Puritans would often distinguish between "union" and "communion." They used the word *union* to describe the unchanging love God has for us when we enter into his family. It is objective and stable, like my being the son of my parents, and we treasure it because it never varies. *Communion* was used to describe our often-changing experience of this relationship with God—much closer to the way we'll be using the word *union* in this book.

6. See Thomas Merton, *New Seeds of Contemplation* (New York: New Directions, 2007), 237.

7. Frederick Dale Bruner, *Matthew: A Commentary*, vol. 1, *The Christbook: Matthew 1–12*, rev. ed. (Grand Rapids, MI: Wm. B. Eerdmans, 2004), 83.

8. Benedict J. Groeschel, *Stumbling Blocks or Stepping Stones: Spiritual Answers to Psychological Questions* (Mahwah, NJ: Paulist Press, 1987), 108.

9. Benedict J. Groeschel, *The Reform of Renewal* (San Francisco: Ignatius Press, 1990), 199.

10. Dallas Willard, *The Spirit of the Disciplines: Understanding How God Changes Lives* (New York: HarperSanFrancisco, 1988), 32.

CHAPTER 4: AWAKENING: SEEING GOD EVERYWHERE

1. Frederick Buechner, *Telling the Truth: The Gospel as Tragedy, Comedy, and Fairy Tale* (New York: HarperSanFrancisco, 1977), 75.

2. M. Robert Mulholland Jr., *Invitation to a Journey: A Road Map for Spiritual Formation*, expanded by Ruth Haley Barton (Downers Grove, IL: InterVarsity Press, 2016), chapter 8.

3. Dallas Willard, *The Divine Conspiracy: Rediscovering Our Hidden Life in God* (New York: HarperSanFrancisco, 1998), 66.

4. William James, *The Varieties of Religious Experience* (The Modern Library, 1902), 8, quoted at Bill Leonard, "Dull Habit or Acute Fever? William James and the Protestant Conversion Crisis," *Harvard Divinity Bulletin*, Summer/Autumn 2015, https://bulletin.hds.harvard.edu/articles/summerautumn2015/dull-habit-or-acute-fever.

5. Leonard, "Dull Habit or Acute Fever?"

6. James L. Crenshaw, *Urgent Advice and Probing Questions: Collected Writings on Old Testament Wisdom* (Macon, GA: Mercer University Press, 1995), 292–93.

7. Charles Taylor, *A Secular Age* (Cambridge, MA: Belknap Press, 2007), chapter 15.

8. Ibid., 5.

9. C. S. Lewis, *The Weight of Glory and Other Addresses* (New York: HarperOne, 1980), 31–32.

10. Gloria Steinem, "Anne Lamott Talks to Gloria Steinem about Writing, Kindness, and Making Sense of the Universe," *Cosmopolitan*, April 3, 2017, http://www.cosmopolitan.com/lifestyle/a9224345/anne-lamott-gloria-steinem-hallelujah-anyway/.

11. Evelyn Underhill, *Mysticism: A Study in the Nature and Development of Spiritual Consciousness* (Mineola, NY: Dover Publications, 2002), 176.

12. Willard, *The Divine Conspiracy*, 61–62.

13. Alcoholics Anonymous, *Twelve Steps and Twelve Traditions* (New York: The A. A. Grapevine and Alcoholics Anonymous World Services, 1981), 106–7.

14. See chapter 7 in Bill J. Leonard, *A Sense of the Heart: Christian Religious Experience in the United States* (Nashville: Abingdon, 2014). Emphasis added.

15. Lewis, *The Weight of Glory*, 36, 42–43.

16. Thomas Merton, "The Night Spirit and the Dawn Air," in *Conjectures of a Guilty Bystander* (New York: Image Books, 1968), 167.

CHAPTER 5: PURGATION: LEAVING BAGGAGE BEHIND

1. Søren Kierkegaard, *The Sickness unto Death: A Christian Psychological Exposition of Edification and Awakening by Anti-Climacus* (London: Penguin Books, 1989), 84.

2. Ibid., 126.

3. Ibid., 109 (emphasis added).

4. Ibid., 115.

5. Quoted in Terre Spencer, "It's Hard to Get Enough of What *Almost* Works," http://www.jungatlanta.com/articles/summer11-hungry-ghosts.pdf.

6. Kent Dunnington, *Addiction and Virtue: Beyond the Models of Disease and Choice* (Downers Grove, IL: InterVarsity Press, 2011), 186–87.

7. Herman Melville, *Moby-Dick* (Boston: C. H. Simonds Company, 1892), 49.

8. David Brooks, *The Road to Character* (New York: Random House, 2015), 6–7.

9. C. S. Lewis, *Mere Christianity* (San Francisco: HarperOne, 2001), 122–24.

10. Cornelius Plantinga Jr., *Not the Way It's Supposed to Be: A Breviary of Sin* (Grand Rapids, MI: Eerdmans, 1995), 82–83.

11. Charles Taylor, *A Secular Age* (Cambridge, MA: Harvard University Press, 2009), 620.

12. James K. A. Smith, *How (Not) to Be Secular: Reading Charles Taylor* (Grand Rapids, MI: Eerdmans, 2014), 107.

13. Dallas Willard, *Renovation of the Heart: Putting On the Character of Christ* (Colorado Springs, CO: NavPress, 2012), 60.

14. Dallas Willard, quoted in Gary Moon's unpublished manuscript.

15. George MacDonald, *Knowing the Heart of God: Where Obedience Is the One Path to Drawing Intuitively Close to Our Father* (Minneapolis: Bethany House, 1990), 52.

16. Dallas Willard, *The Divine Conspiracy: Rediscovering Our Hidden Life in God* (New York: HarperSanFrancisco, 1998), 342.

17. Plantinga, *Not the Way It's Supposed to Be*, 34.

18. Interestingly, the Septuagint—the ancient Greek translation of the Old Testament—often uses cognates of *hygiano* to translate *shalom*, a word that we usually translate as "peace" but that has a much richer meaning, closer to wholeness.

19. Plantinga, *Not the Way It's Supposed to Be*, 35.

CHAPTER 6: ILLUMINATION: A NEW MENTAL MAP

1. Helen Keller, *The Story of My Life*, ed. John Albert Macy (New York: Grosset and Dunlap, 1905), 21.

2. Ibid., 23–24.

3. Lewis Carroll, *Through the Looking-Glass*, chapter 5.

4. Richard B. Hays, *The Faith of Jesus Christ: The Narrative Substructure of Galatians 3:1–4:11* (Grand Rapids, MI: Eerdmans, 2002), 148–50.

5. Matthew 16:16 in *Da Jesus Book* (Orlando: Wycliffe Bible Translators, 2000).

CHAPTER 7: UNION: NEVER ALONE

1. Amanda White, "Smells Ring Bells: How Smell Triggers Memories and Emotions," *Brain Babble* (blog), January 12, 2015, https://www.psychologytoday.com/blog/brain-babble/201501/smells-ring-bells-how-smell-triggers-memories-and-emotions.

2. Quoted in Terre Spencer, "It's Hard to Get Enough of What *Almost* Works," http://www.jungatlanta.com/articles/summer11-hungry-ghosts.pdf.

3. Erwin Schrödinger, *What Is Life?: With Mind and Matter and Autobiographical Sketches* (Cambridge, UK: Cambridge University Press, 1992), 69.

4. Dallas Willard, *The Spirit of the Disciplines: Understanding How God Changes Lives* (New York: HarperSanFrancisco, 1988), 57.

5. Christopher J. H. Wright, *Salvation Belongs to Our God: Celebrating the Bible's Central Story* (Downers Grove, IL: InterVarsity Press, 2007), 43.

6. Rankin Wilbourne, *Union with Christ: The Way to Know and Enjoy God* (Colorado Springs: David C. Cook, 2016).

7. John Calvin, *Institutes of the Christian Religion*, II.xvii.1.

8. Huston Smith, *The World's Religions* (New York: HarperCollins, 1991), 115.

9. Mallory Ortberg, "Ayn Rand Reviews Children's Movies," *The New Yorker*, December 18, 2014, https://www.newyorker.com/humor/daily-shouts/ayn-rand-reviews-childrens-movies.

10. C. S. Lewis, *The Weight of Glory and Other Addresses* (New York: Macmillan, 1980), 16–17.

11. Brenda B. Colijn, *Images of Salvation in the New Testament* (Downers Grove, IL: InterVarsity Press, 2010), 249.

12. Luke Timothy Johnson, foreword to *The Faith of Christ: The Narrative Substructure of Galatians 3:1–4:11*, by Richard B. Hays (Grand Rapids, MI: Eerdmans, 2002), xiv.

13. Klyne Snodgrass, *Who God Says You Are* (Grand Rapids, MI: Eerdmans, 2018), 94–95.

14. Miroslav Volf, *Exclusion and Embrace: A Theological Exploration of Identity, Otherness, and Reconciliation* (Nashville: Abingdon, 1996), 69.

15. C. S. Lewis, *Mere Christianity* (New York: HarperCollins, 1952), 63–64.

16. Ibid., 175–77.

17. *Jesus: An Experiment in Christology* (New York: Crossroad, 1981), 201.

ABOUT THE AUTHOR

John Ortberg is an author, a speaker, and the senior pastor of Menlo Church in the San Francisco Bay Area. A consistent theme of John's teaching is how to follow a Jesus way of life— that is, how faith in Christ can affect our everyday lives with God. His books include *All the Places to Go . . . How Will You Know?*, *Soul Keeping*, *Who Is This Man?*, *The Life You've Always Wanted*, *Faith and Doubt*, and *If You Want to Walk on Water, You've Got to Get Out of the Boat*. John teaches around the world at conferences and churches.

Born and raised in Rockford, Illinois, John graduated from Wheaton College. He holds a master's of divinity and a doctorate in clinical psychology from Fuller Seminary, and he did postgraduate work at the University of Aberdeen, Scotland.

John is a member of the board of trustees at Fuller Seminary, where he has also served as an adjunct faculty member. He is on the board of the Dallas Willard Center for Spiritual Formation and has served in the past on the board of Christianity Today International.

Now that their children are grown, John and his wife, Nancy, enjoy surfing in the Pacific to help care for their souls. He can be followed on Twitter @johnortberg.

JOIN JOHN ORTBERG ON THIS 5-SESSION
JOURNEY TO DISCOVER WHAT IT
REALLY MEANS TO BE SAVED.

Great for small-
group or individual
Bible study.

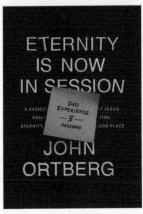

DVD to accompany
the participant's
guide, with teaching
from John Ortberg.

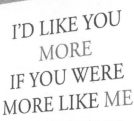

MARTIN INSTITUTE
for Christianity and Culture
WESTMONT COLLEGE

The Martin Institute for Christianity and Culture is dedicated to placing an enduring emphasis on spiritual formation with a particular focus on the path of authentic transformation as an interactive, loving relationship with Jesus Christ. As part of that quest, we hope to honor the legacy of Dallas Willard while placing his work in the context of other thought and praxis leaders who have developed methods for authentic Christian formation that have stood the test of time.

The Goals:

The goals of the Martin Institute for Christianity and Culture are to 1) support a new generation of thought leaders in the area of Christian spiritual formation and 2) help establish this discipline as a domain of public knowledge that is open to research and pedagogy of the highest order.

The Centers:

Dallas Willard Research Center: Supports and engages in Christian spiritual formation research and writing efforts through 1) maintaining and offering access to the books and papers of Dallas Willard's personal library, including online availability for many of these resources; 2) a senior fellows program; 3) annual book and research awards programs; and 4) providing faculty research retreats.

Conversatio Divina: A Center for Spiritual Renewal: Creates and offers resources for both "pilgrims" and "guides." Specific activities include 1) academic course development for pastors, church leaders, spiritual directors, and mental health professionals; 2) development of small group curriculum projects in the area of spiritual formation; 3) a variety of writing efforts; and 4) continuing education and retreat offerings for ministry leaders.

Westmont Center for Spiritual Formation: Offers spiritual formation opportunities for the Westmont community through providing a retreat space and programming along with partnerships across campus. Specific offerings include small group development, residence-life-based spiritual formation coordinators, and support for Augustinian Scholars and chapel programs.

For more information, visit www.dallaswillardcenter.com.

CP1383